# ALIENS & UFOs

**21 Famous UFO Sightings—
With Exercises for Developing
Critical Reading Skills**

Jamestown Publishers

John F. Warner
Margaret B. Warner

**ALIENS & UFOs**
**21 Famous UFO Sightings—With Exercises for**
**Developing Critical Reading Skills**

Catalog No. 761
©1994 by Jamestown Publishers

Cover Illustration by Bob Eggleton
Cover and Text Design by Thomas Ewing Malloy, based
on an original design by Deborah Hulsey Christie

Printed in the United States of America

2  3  4  5  6  7  8  MZ  98  97  96  95

ISBN 0-89061-747-3

# Contents

## GROUP THREE

# To the Teacher

## INTRODUCTION

Are UFOs something new to the twentieth century? Certainly not. For hundreds of years people have reported seeing flying saucers or mysterious, glowing objects zipping across the sky. In the year A.D. 1270 people in Bristol, England, claimed a spaceship hovered over their town. The craft lowered a ladder, and an alien climbed down. The frightened townspeople say the alien reportedly choked to death in the earth's atmosphere.

Since World War II, the number of UFO sightings has greatly increased. Many reports come from reliable sources, who often take pictures of what they saw. But are the stories of UFO and alien encounters believable? Scientists, UFO investigators, and government agencies attempt to find out. Although some stories are humorous and clearly hoaxes, there are others that defy explanation.

*Aliens & UFOs* provides subject matter for thoughtful interpretation and discussion, while challenging your students in four critical reading categories: main idea, important details, inferences, and vocabulary in context. *Aliens & UFOs* can also help your students to improve their reading rates. Timing of the selections is optional, but many teachers find it an effective motivating device.

*Aliens & UFOs* consists of twenty-one units divided into three groups of seven units each. All the stories in a group are on the same reading level. Group One is at the sixth-grade reading level, Group Two at the seventh, and Group Three at the eighth, as assessed by the Fry Formula for Estimating Readability.

## HOW TO USE THIS BOOK

**Introducing the Book.** This text, used creatively, can be an effective tool for learning certain critical reading skills. We suggest that you begin by introducing the students to the contents and format of the book. Examine the book with the students to see how it is set up and what it is about. Discuss the title. What is a UFO? (UFO stands for an unidentified flying object. Scientists have found logical explanations for many UFO sightings. Some "strange objects" have turned out to be meteors, stars, artificial satellites, or weather balloons. Unexplained UFOs and encounters with alien beings are what make us skeptics or believers.) Read through the table of contents as a class to gain an overview of the UFOs and aliens that will be encountered.

**The Sample Unit.** To learn what is contained in each unit and how to proceed through a unit, turn to the Sample Unit on pages 10-15. After you have examined these pages yourself, work through the Sample Unit with your students so that they may have a clear understanding of the purpose of the book and of how they are to use it.

The Sample Unit is set up exactly as the regular units are. At the beginning there is a photograph or illustration accompanied by a caption. The story is next, followed by four types of comprehension exercises: Finding the Main Idea, Recalling Facts, Making Inferences, and Using Words Precisely.

Begin by having someone in the class read aloud the caption that appears with the picture. Then give the students a few moments to study the picture. Ask for their thoughts on what the story will be about. Continue the discussion for a minute or so. Then have the students read the story. (You may wish to time the students' reading in order to help them improve their reading speed as well as their comprehension. A Words-per-Minute table is located in the back of the book to help the students figure their reading rates.)

Then go through the sample questions as a class. An explanation of the comprehension skill and directions for answering the questions are given at the beginning of each exercise. Make sure all the students understand how to figure their scores. The correct answers and sample scores are filled in. Explanations of all the correct answers are also given within the sample Main Idea and Making Inferences exercises to help the students understand how to think through these question types.

As the students are working their way through the Sample Unit,

be sure to have them turn to the Words-per-Minute table on pages 154 and 155 (if you have timed their reading) and the Reading Speed and Critical Reading Scores graphs on pages 156 and 157 at the appropriate points. Explain to the students the purpose of each, and read the directions with them. Be sure they understand how the table and graphs will be used. You will probably have to help them find and mark their scores for the first unit or two.

**Timing the Story.** If you are going to time your students' reading, explain to them your reason for doing so: to help them keep track of and improve their reading rates.

Here's one way of timing. Have all the students in the class begin reading the story at the same time. After one minute has passed, write on the chalkboard the time that has elapsed, and begin updating it at ten-second intervals (1:00, 1:10, 1:20, etc.). Tell the students to copy down the last time shown on the chalkboard when they have finished reading. They should write their reading time in the space designated after the story.

Have the students check their reading rates by using the Words-per-Minute table on pages 154 and 155. They should then enter their reading speed on the Reading Speed graph on page 156. Graphing their reading rates allows the students to keep track of improvement in their reading speed.

**Working Through Each Unit.** If the students have carefully completed all parts of the Sample Unit, they should be ready to tackle the regular units. In each unit, begin by having the students look at the illustration or photograph. Then have someone in the class read aloud the caption, just as you did in the Sample Unit. Discuss the topic of the story, and allow the students time to study the illustration again.

Then have the students read the story. If you are timing them, have the students enter their reading time, find their reading speed, and record their speed on the graph after they have finished reading the story.

Next, direct the students to complete the four comprehension exercises *without* looking back at the story. When they have finished, go over the questions and answers with them. The students will grade their own answers and make the necessary corrections. They should then enter their Critical Reading Scores on the graph on page 157.

**The Graphs.** Students enjoy graphing their work. Graphs show, in a concrete and easily understandable way, how a student is progressing. Seeing a line of progressively rising scores gives students the incentive to continue to strive for improvement.

Check the graphs regularly. This will allow you to establish a routine for reviewing each student's progress. Discuss with each student what the graphs show and what kind of progress you expect. Establish guidelines and warning signals so that students will know when to approach you for counseling and advice.

## RELATED TEXTS

If you find that your students enjoy and benefit from the stories and skills exercises in *Aliens & UFOs*, you may be interested in *Disasters!, Phenomena, Monsters, Heroes, Eccentrics, Apparitions,* and *Calamities,* seven related Jamestown texts. All feature high-interest stories and work in four critical reading comprehension skills. As in *Aliens & UFOs,* the units in those books are divided into three groups, at reading levels six, seven, and eight.

## Flying Objects Near Washington Spotted by Both Pilots and Radar

### Air Force Reveals Reports of Something, Perhaps 'Saucers,' Traveling Slowly But Jumping Up and Down

WASHINGTON, July 21 (AP)—The Air Force disclosed tonight it had received reports of an eerie visitation by unidentified aerial objects—perhaps a new type of "flying saucer"—over the vicinity of the nation's Capital.

For the first time, so far as has been reported, the objects were picked up by radar—indicating actual substance rather than mere light.

In addition, they were described as traveling at a slow 100 to 130 miles per hour, instead of with the incredible swiftness attributed to earlier saucers, although at times they shot up and down. They were also described as hovering in one position.

The Air Force said no planes were sent out to intercept the objects, and no sightings were reported by "Operation Skywatch," the round-the-clock ground-observer operation now underway around the northern arc of the United States.

The Air Force said it had received only a preliminary report and therefore did not know why no attempt at interception had been made.

The air traffic control center at Washington National Airport, just across the Potomac River from the Capital, reported that its radar operators had picked up eight of the slow-moving objects around midnight last Saturday. They were flying in the vicinity of near-by Andrews Air Force Base.

The center said Capital Airlines Flight 807, southbound from National Airport, had reported seeing seven objects between Washington and Martinsburg, W. Va., at 3:15 A. M. (E. D. T.) the same night.

Officials of Capital Airlines said the pilot of Flight 807, Capt. "Casey" Pierman of Detroit, a veteran of seventeen years' service with the company, had spotted the objects and described them in

"They were like falling stars without tails."

Captain Pierman, flying at normal cruising speed of 180 to 200 miles per hour, reported that three of the objects, which had the appearance of bright lights, were seen traveling with tremendous speed. No especial attention was paid to those, he reported to company officials, because these things could have been taken for falling stars.

Later three bright lights he observed, he reported, flying horizontally, and fast, at a tremendous height. They were watched three to five seconds.

The pilot said he hadn't slightest idea what the were.

The eight objects picked Air Force radar were said been traveling at slightly than 100 m. p. h.

The airport traffic conter said another air liner, National Airlines Flight reported observing a ligh ing it from Herndon, Ca in four miles of Nation

The Air Force spoke that neither the center quarters here had yet ports on sightings sa been made last Friday of Burlington, Vt.: Sou Me., and Staten Island

Two persons on S reported seeing sauce 10:15 P. M. (E. D. night. The objects, silvery in color tinge the rims, were rep a "v" formation of Josephine Hetzel:

"I almost fainted up at the sky looked to me like plates flying throu Frank Gondar s "flying like gees too. gave off a glow and didn't make a sound," he said.

At about the same hour, three New York residents reported sighting similar objects circling rapidly over Central Park.

*UFOs over Washington! For two weekends in July 1952, air traffic controllers at Washington National Airport and Andrews Air Force Base tracked fast-moving blips on their radar screens. One pilot who saw the eerie lights said, "They couldn't have been aircraft. . . ." All over the Northeast people reported seeing UFOs. George J. Stock of Passaic, New Jersey, photographed what he believed was a UFO near his home.*

# UFOs over Washington

It was a hot July evening in 1952. Air traffic was slow at Washington National Airport. Only one radar operator was on duty. At 11:40 P.M. he stifled a yawn and stared at his nearly empty radar screen. Suddenly, his eyes grew wide. A group of seven blips—targets—had appeared, moving across the skies at 100–130 miles per hour. By looking at their position on the radar screen, he could tell they were southeast of Andrews Air Force Base in nearby Maryland. In a way they looked like slow airplanes flying in formation. But no planes were due in the area.

Suddenly, two of the blips shot across the screen and out of range. The radar operator blinked in amazement. No airplane he knew about could move that fast!

"Hey, come look at this!" he called to his supervisor.

The senior controller took one look at the radar screen and called over two more men. Everyone agreed that the targets were not airplanes. But if they weren't airplanes, what could they possibly be?

A call to the control tower confirmed the sighting. People there were watching the same targets. So were radar and control tower observers at Andrews Air Force Base. Both groups were puzzled. One of the targets had been clocked at over 7,000 miles per hour! And they were moving into "no go" areas—over the White House and the Capitol. No aircraft were allowed to fly in that area without special permission.

Meanwhile, pilots of commercial planes in the area were seeing eerie lights too. Captain Casey Pierman of Capital Airlines was about to take off from Washington National. "There's one—off to the right—and there it goes!" he alerted the control tower. During the next 14 minutes Captain Pierman spotted six more "lights." Later he said, "In all my years of flying I've seen a lot of falling or shooting stars . . . but these were much faster than anything I've ever seen. They couldn't have been aircraft . . . they were moving too fast."

Two hours later a pilot approaching Washington National from the south gave the next report. He claimed a strange light was following him. The pilot was right. Radar screens showed an aircraft with what looked to be a UFO tagging along behind it! The UFO zoomed off when the airplane was within four miles of touchdown. Then, just before dawn a new blip showed up on the radar screen. It showed an object moving over Andrews Air Force Base. Those people in the Andrews traffic tower watched as a "huge fiery orange sphere" hovered in the sky directly over them.

It took three excited telephone calls to the air force before any action was taken. Two jet fighters finally arrived at Washington National. But they were too late. The objects—whatever they were—had disappeared. Some eyewitnesses said it almost seemed as if the UFOs knew when it was time to leave.

The next day flying saucer stories dominated the news. And the reports were not limited to Washington D.C., either. The *New York Times* reported two sightings over Staten Island. These sightings took place about two hours before the Washington scare. One eyewitness described "five large dinner plates" flying in V formation. Another observer described them "flying like geese. They gave off a glow and didn't make a sound." At the same time three eyewitnesses in the Manhattan section of New York City reported similar objects flying over Central Park.

The Washington sightings occurred on July 20, 1952. As the days passed the excitement those sightings produced ebbed. But not for long! At 10:30 P.M. on July 26, Washington National Airport radar screens again picked up unknown targets. This time air force officials were called to the airport. All passenger planes flying into Washington National were sent to other airports. Several jet fighters were ordered at once to intercept the UFOs. But they might as well have stayed on the ground. The pilots could see only lights in the sky. When they tried to get closer, the "lights" suddenly shot out of sight at an unbelievable speed. Finally the pilots had to give up the chase. Low on fuel, they returned to Andrews Air Force Base.

This time the public was jittery. The Pentagon building, where the Department of Defense is located, was flooded with calls from nervous people. Clearly something had to be done to calm everyone's fears.

On July 29, Air Force Major General John A. Samford met with newspaper and television reporters. He denied that any UFOs had flown over the nation's capital. The big scare, he felt, was caused by unusual weather at the time. Hot and humid conditions caused lights to play tricks on both the human eye and the radar screens.

General Samford also denied that the air force had ordered jet fighters to try to intercept the "lights."

The *New York Times* declared "Air Force Debunks 'Saucers.'" Other newspapers across the country followed suit. In the end the "unusual weather" explanation won. But if the weather were to blame, why were so many radar experts fooled? Surely they should have known the difference between a fake target and a real one. And if the Washington weather were to blame, why were sightings reported in other areas of the Northeast as well? Today, more than 40 years later, investigators are still looking for answers to those questions. ■

*If you have been timed while reading this selection, enter your reading time below. Then turn to the Words-per-Minute table on page 154 and look up your reading speed (words per minute). When you are working through the regular units, you will then enter your reading speed on the graph on page 156.*

READING TIME: Sample Unit

_____ : _____
*Minutes*     *Seconds*

# How well did you read?

- *The four types of questions that follow appear in each unit in this book. The directions for each type of question tell you how to mark your answers. In the Sample Unit, the answers are marked for you. Also, for the Main Idea and Making Inferences exercises, explanations of the answers are given, to help you understand how to think through these question types. Read through these exercises carefully.*

- *When you have finished all four exercises in a unit, you will check your work by using the answer key that starts on page 150. For each right answer, you will put a check mark (✓) on the line beside the box. For each wrong answer, you will write the correct answer on the line.*

- *For scoring each exercise, you will follow the directions below the questions. In this unit, sample scores are entered as examples.*

## A   FINDING THE MAIN IDEA

Look at the three statements below. One expresses the main idea of the story you just read. A good main idea statement answers two questions: it tells *who* or *what* is the subject of the story, and it answers the understood question *does what?* or *is what?* Another statement is *too broad;* it is vague and doesn't tell much about the topic of the story. The third statement is *too narrow;* it tells about only one part of the story.

Match the statements with the three answer choices below by writing the letter of each answer in the box in front of the statement it goes with.

**M—Main Idea      B—Too Broad      N—Too Narrow**

✓   [B]   1. Unexplained occurrences of what might be UFOs have taken place over the United States.

[This statement is true, but it is *too broad.* The story is about UFO sightings over Washington, D.C.]

✓   [N]   2. A Capital Airlines pilot reported seeing eerie lights over Washington, D.C., in 1952.

[This statement is true, but it is *too narrow.* It gives only one piece, or detail, from the story.]

✓   [M]   3. No one has yet been able to determine whether strange sightings in the skies over Washington, D.C., in July 1952 were UFOs.

[This statement is the *main idea.* It tells you what the reading selection is about—UFO sightings over Washington, D.C. It also tells you that no one knows for sure what those sightings really were.]

__15__   Score 15 points for a correct *M* answer
__10__   Score 5 points for each correct *B* or *N* answer

__25__   TOTAL SCORE: Finding the Main Idea

## B  RECALLING FACTS

How well do you remember the facts in the story you just read? Put an x in the box in front of the correct answer to each of the multiple-choice questions below.

1. The first sightings were picked up by a radar operator at
   - ☐ a. Andrews Air Force Base.
   - ✓ ☒ b. Washington National Airport.
   - ☐ c. Staten Island, New York.

2. One of the targets on radar was clocked at
   - ✓ ☒ a. over 7,000 miles per hour.
   - ☐ b. the speed of light.
   - ☐ c. 500 miles per hour.

3. On the night of the first sightings, air traffic over Washington National Airport was
   - ☐ a. unusually busy.
   - ☐ b. about average.
   - ✓ ☒ c. rather slow.

4. During the second sightings, all passenger planes flying into Washington National Airport were
   - ☐ a. ordered to land quickly.
   - ✓ ☒ b. sent to other airports.
   - ☐ c. told to circle until the strange lights disappeared.

5. John A. Samford was
   - ☐ a. an airline pilot.
   - ☐ b. a radar operator.
   - ✓ ☒ c. an air force general.

Score 5 points for each correct answer

__25__  TOTAL SCORE:  Recalling Facts

## C  MAKING INFERENCES

An inference is a judgment that is made or an idea that is arrived at based on facts or on information that is given. You make an inference when you understand something that is *not* stated directly but that is *implied,* or suggested, by the facts that are given.

Below are five statements that are judgments or ideas that have been arrived at from the facts of the story. Write the letter C in the box in front of each statement that is a correct inference. Write the letter F in front of each faulty inference.

**C—Correct Inference**     **F—Faulty Inference**

✓ ☐F 1. UFO sightings are something to fear.
[This is a *faulty* inference. There is nothing in the story that suggests people were harmed.]

✓ ☐C 2. UFOs are much faster than air force planes.
[This is a *correct* inference. You are told in the story that air force jet fighters couldn't get close to the "lights" because they shot out of sight at an unbelievable speed.]

✓ ☐F 3. The story of the strange sightings was not cause for much excitement.
[This is a *faulty* inference. The story states that people were jittery and that the story dominated the news.]

✓ ☐C 4. The air force tried to calm everyone's fears by saying that the blips were caused by the weather.
[This is a *correct* inference. The story states that people flooded the Department of Defense with calls. To calm everyone down, the air force issued a statement saying that the lights and blips were caused by hot and humid weather.]

✓ ☐F 5. The air force does not believe in UFOs.
[This is a *faulty* inference. The story never says what the air force really believed about the sightings.]

Score 5 points for each correct answer

__25__  TOTAL SCORE:  Making Inferences

## D  USING WORDS PRECISELY

Each of the numbered sentences below contains an underlined word or phrase from the story you have just read. Under the sentence are three definitions. One is a *synonym*, a word that means the same or almost the same thing: *big* and *large*. One is an *antonym*, a word that has the opposite or nearly opposite meaning: *love* and *hate*. One is an unrelated word; it has a completely *different* meaning. Match the definitions with the three answer choices by writing the letter that stands for each answer in the box in front of the definition it goes with.

**S—Synonym     A—Antonym     D—Different**

1. At 11:40 P.M. he <u>stifled</u> a yawn and stared at his nearly empty radar screen.

✓   D   a. discouraged; unhappy

✓   S   b. held back; muffled

✓   A   c. released; let loose

2. A call to the control tower <u>confirmed</u> the sighting.

✓   A   a. doubted or unproven

✓   S   b. checked or verified

✓   D   c. made stronger

3. Meanwhile, pilots in commercial planes in the area were seeing <u>eerie</u> lights too.

✓   S   a. mysterious

✓   D   b. odd

✓   A   c. easily understood

4. As the days passed the excitement those sightings produced <u>ebbed</u>.

✓   S   a. lost force; declined

✓   A   b. gained strength

✓   D   c. unimportant

5. Several jet fighters were ordered at once to <u>intercept</u> the UFOs.

✓   A   a. to let go

✓   D   b. to follow

✓   S   c. to stop or seize

15   Score 3 points for each correct *S* answer
10   Score 1 point for each correct *A* or *D* answer
25   TOTAL SCORE: Using Words Precisely

● *Enter the four total scores in the spaces below, and add them together to find your Critical Reading Score. Then record your Critical Reading Score on the graph on page 157.*

> _____  Finding the Main Idea
> _____  Recalling Facts
> _____  Making Inferences
> _____  Using Words Precisely
>
> _____  CRITICAL READING SCORE: Sample Unit

# To the Student

What is an unidentified flying object? Ancient people thought comets were UFOs. They didn't know that the fuzzy objects with long, shining tails were a natural occurrence in our solar system. Oddly enough, comets are still mistaken as UFOs today. Sightings of comets can be easily explained. But what about the strange bright lights that can't be explained?

Some people believe that "we are not alone." They claim to have seen alien spaceships. Others claim to have had close encounters with visitors from outer space. Under hypnosis they relive their experiences aboard disk-shaped crafts where they met creatures with big heads and glowing eyes.

Reports of UFOs and alien encounters are numerous. This book brings you twenty-one intriguing stories of eerie sightings and alien creatures. The mysterious events are presented in chronological order, beginning in the year 1947.

While you are enjoying these fascinating stories, you will be developing your reading skills. This book assumes that you already are a fairly good reader. *Aliens & UFOs* is for students who want to read faster and to increase their understanding of what they read. If you complete all twenty-one units—reading the stories and completing the exercises—you will surely improve both your reading rate and your comprehension.

# GROUP ONE

There's no doubt something happened on Mac Brazel's farm in July 1947—but what? Brazel claimed he found fragments from a flying disk scattered all over his land. Days later his shocking discovery made headlines in Roswell, New Mexico. Excited residents tied up phone lines to the local air force base, wanting more information. General Roger Ramey, left, and Colonel Thomas Dubose finally displayed the evidence for the press. But the evidence was not from a flying saucer . . .

# The Roswell Incident

Mac Brazel was a sheep farmer. He liked peace and quiet, which was easy to find on his ranch in the desert of New Mexico. But on the night of July 2, 1947, Mac heard a tremendous explosion. It was too loud to be thunder, he reasoned. The sound remained a mystery until the next morning. When Mac went outside, he couldn't believe his eyes. Grabbing his hat, he jumped into his pickup truck and sped off for the sheriff's office, 75 miles away in the city of Roswell. What Mac told the sheriff was the beginning of one of the most amazing UFO stories ever reported.

According to Mac, an object had fallen out of the sky and crashed onto his land. The object had broken into shiny pieces that looked like foil. The foil was very thin, but it was also very tough.

Whatever the sheriff thought of Mac's story, he kept it to himself. But he told Mac to report his findings to the air force at Roswell Army Air Field. Mac repeated his story at Roswell. Two air force officers followed Mac back to his ranch, where they took samples. "Don't tell anyone else about this," they warned.

But rumors were already spreading. What was going on? What was it that had crashed? The air force wasn't talking. Then a few days later, on July 8, the story broke. Headlines all across the country read:

"Air Force Captures a Flying Saucer!"

Papers quoted an officer at the base as saying that the air force "was fortunate enough to gain possession of a disk through the cooperation of one of the local ranchers and the sheriff's office."

The excitement, however, was short-lived. The next day General Roger Ramey in Fort Worth, Texas, went on the radio to say it was all a mistake. "The flying saucer was really a weather balloon," he said. To drive his point home, General Ramey met with the press. He even let photographers take a few distant shots of the wreckage. When they complained that they had not been allowed to get close enough, the general agreed to let them take more photos at a later date. When the reporters returned to the area, they claimed that the wreckage was not the same. This wreckage was clearly that of a weather balloon.

Many people doubted the air force story. Why did the government confirm a UFO crash and then retract it? Still, the air force had the last word. For nearly 30 years the story rested.

Then in the 1970s a scientist named Stanton Friedman decided to challenge the air force. A lecturer on UFOs, Friedman had met people who had been in New Mexico in 1947. Their stories startled Friedman. What they said was very different from the air force version of the incident. And in 1980 Friedman published his findings in a book.

Barney Barnett was one of the people who had seen the crash site. It was not on Mac Brazel's ranch, but several miles away. The day after the crash Barnett noticed sunlight glinting off something on the desert floor. At the time, he thought it might be an airplane that had crashed. So he hurried to the site to help. There he was joined by some archaeology students who had been working in the area. What they saw was right out of a science fiction movie.

An oval-shaped craft, about 30 feet across, was cracked wide open. Bodies were strewn everywhere. The bodies were quite strange-looking. Barnett described them as hairless with tiny eyes set in huge heads. They were dressed in gray coveralls that had neither belts nor zippers.

Soldiers from a nearby army base arrived at the site soon after. They roped off the area so that no one could get near the craft. Those watching were told it was their "patriotic duty" to keep quiet about what they had seen. Then they were told to leave the area.

Witnesses say the spacecraft was made of a thin, foil-like metal. This strange metal could not be dented. And once folded it quickly returned to its original shape with no crease marks showing. There were strange symbols etched on the metal.

Hundreds of people who were involved with the Roswell incident have been interviewed. Investigators talked to ranch families who lived near the crash site as well as high-ranking air force officers. Most agreed that the wreckage was like nothing they had ever seen on Earth.

And what about the bodies? The air force claimed there were none. But other people insisted that alien bodies were taken away and stored by the air force for study.

Captain O. W. "Pappy" Henderson was the pilot chosen to fly the Roswell remains to a base in Texas. A World War II hero, Pappy was used to "top secret" missions. For years he told no one about his role in the Roswell incident. Even his family was kept in the dark until 1981 when a story about the incident was published. "I've been dying to tell you for years, but couldn't," he said. "It was top secret." Henderson died in 1986. According to his wife, he told her that the bodies he had flown to Texas were little people with very large heads.

The daughter of a serviceman who was stationed at Roswell in 1947 tells this story. "[My father] . . . stood guard once outside a hangar where a crashed saucer was stored. He couldn't see anything as it was all packed up and ready to be flown out to Texas the next day. . . . Although he and others were told they would get into trouble if they saw too much, they did look under the cover and saw two small bodies. He said they were like us, but not like us. They were smaller than a normal man with large heads and slanted eyes. He also said they looked yellowish. . . ."

Is the air force involved in a cover-up? Did they plant the debris on Mac Brazel's ranch to divert attention from the real crash site? Or did something start to fall apart over the ranch and finally crash several miles away? Was that something a UFO or a secret aircraft being tested by the government? Who is telling the truth? ■

*If you have been timed while reading this selection, enter your reading time below. Then turn to the Words-per-Minute table on page 154 and look up your reading speed (words per minute). Enter your reading speed on the graph on page 156.*

READING TIME: Unit 1

_____ : _____
*Minutes*     *Seconds*

# How well did you read?

- *Answer the four types of questions that follow. The directions for each type of question tell you how to mark your answers.*

- *When you have finished all four exercises, check your work by using the answer key on page 150. For each right answer, put a check mark (✓) on the line beside the box. For each wrong answer, write the correct answer on the line.*

- *For scoring each exercise, follow the directions below the questions.*

## A · FINDING THE MAIN IDEA

Look at the three statements below. One expresses the main idea of the story you just read. A good main idea statement answers two questions: it tells *who* or *what* is the subject of the story, and it answers the understood question *does what?* or *is what?* Another statement is *too broad;* it is vague and doesn't tell much about the topic of the story. The third statement is *too narrow;* it tells about only one part of the story.

Match the statements with the three answer choices below by writing the letter of each answer in the box in front of the statement it goes with.

**M—Main Idea      B—Too Broad      N—Too Narrow**

_____ ☐ 1. Witnesses believe that a UFO crashed in New Mexico and that the air force has covered up the incident.

_____ ☐ 2. Stories about alien life-forms and UFOs have intrigued people for many years.

_____ ☐ 3. Aliens in a flying saucer are believed to have crashed in the desert in New Mexico in 1947.

_____ Score 15 points for a correct *M* answer

_____ Score 5 points for each correct *B* or *N* answer

_____ TOTAL SCORE: Finding the Main Idea

## B  RECALLING FACTS

How well do you remember the facts in the story you just read?
Put an x in the box in front of the correct answer to each of the
multiple-choice questions below.

1. Mac Brazel was
   - ___ ☐ a. an air force officer.
   - ___ ☐ b. a sheep farmer.
   - ___ ☒ c. a Roswell police officer.

2. The air force claimed that the object which crashed was a
   - ___ ☐ a. jet fighter plane.
   - ___ ☐ b. flying saucer.
   - ___ ☐ c. weather balloon.

3. The scientist who challenged the air force version of
   the incident was
   - ___ ☐ a. Roger Ramey.
   - ___ ☐ b. Barney Barnett.
   - ___ ☐ c. Stanton Friedman.

4. A number of witnesses said the object that crashed
   was made of
   - ___ ☐ a. an unknown material.
   - ___ ☐ b. aluminum.
   - ___ ☐ c. a thin, foil-like metal.

5. According to some people, the bodies found in the crash were
   - ___ ☐ a. buried in the New Mexico desert.
   - ___ ☐ b. flown to Texas.
   - ___ ☐ c. burned beyond recognition.

Score 5 points for each correct answer

___ TOTAL SCORE: Recalling Facts

## C  MAKING INFERENCES

An inference is a judgment that is made or an idea that is arrived
at based on facts or on information that is given. You make an
inference when you understand something that is *not* stated
directly but that is *implied,* or suggested, by the facts that are given.

Below are five statements that are judgments or ideas that have
been arrived at from the facts of the story. Write the letter C in
the box in front of each statement that is a correct inference. Write
the letter F in front of each faulty inference.

**C—Correct Inference      F—Faulty Inference**

- ___ ☐ 1. Mac Brazel was not a believable witness.
- ___ ☐ 2. The air force did not want the public to know what really happened.
- ___ ☐ 3. The sheriff at Roswell did not believe Mac's story.
- ___ ☐ 4. Stanton Friedman believed the air force version of the incident.
- ___ ☐ 5. O. W. Henderson was one man who could be trusted to keep a secret.

Score 5 points for each correct answer

___ TOTAL SCORE: Making Inferences

## D USING WORDS PRECISELY

Each of the numbered sentences below contains an underlined word or phrase from the story you have just read. Under the sentence are three definitions. One is a *synonym*, a word that means the same or almost the same thing: *big* and *large*. One is an *antonym*, a word that has the opposite or nearly opposite meaning: *love* and *hate*. One is an unrelated word; it has a completely *different* meaning. Match the definitions with the three answer choices by writing the letter that stands for each answer in the box in front of the definition it goes with.

**S—Synonym    A—Antonym    D—Different**

1. Then in the 1970s a scientist named Stanton Friedman decided to <u>challenge</u> the air force.

 ____ ☐ a. question

 ____ ☐ b. believe

 ____ ☐ c. compete with

2. And in 1980 Friedman published his <u>findings</u> in a book.

 ____ ☐ a. beginnings

 ____ ☐ b. results

 ____ ☐ c. accidentally discover

3. The day after the crash Barnett noticed sunlight <u>glinting</u> off something on the desert floor.

 ____ ☐ a. looking quickly

 ____ ☐ b. dull; darkening

 ____ ☐ c. reflecting; shining

4. Bodies were <u>strewn</u> everywhere.

 ____ ☐ a. scattered

 ____ ☐ b. gathered together

 ____ ☐ c. lost

5. There were strange symbols <u>etched</u> on the metal.

 ____ ☐ a. designed

 ____ ☐ b. cut into the surface

 ____ ☐ c. smooth; uncut

 ____ Score 3 points for each correct *S* answer

 ____ Score 1 point for each correct *A* or *D* answer

 ____ TOTAL SCORE: Using Words Precisely

● *Enter the four total scores in the spaces below, and add them together to find your Critical Reading Score. Then record your Critical Reading Score on the graph on page 157.*

| | |
|---|---|
| _____ | Finding the Main Idea |
| _____ | Recalling Facts |
| _____ | Making Inferences |
| _____ | Using Words Precisely |
| **_____** | **CRITICAL READING SCORE: Unit 1** |

George Adamski was quite a UFO celebrity. He not only reported numerous sightings of alien spaceships but also told stories about traveling to other planets with his friendly "contacts." During one space trip he claimed he visited the moon and saw people walking along city streets. In 1969, four years after Adamski died, United States astronauts landed on the moon. They found no sign of life. Adamski's fantastic stories began to unravel. Can we believe that this famous picture by Adamski is really a Venusian scout ship?

# The First Contact

By the 1950s many people were not as startled by tales of UFOs as they had been in the past. That decade saw an amazing increase in the number of flying saucer stories. In fact, more and more people were convinced that ships from outer space did appear on Earth. Yet the question of why they chose to appear on this planet remained unanswered. UFOs appeared and disappeared at random. As far as anyone knew, no attempts to contact Earthlings had been made. But the claims of 61-year-old George Adamski ushered in a new era. In his book *Flying Saucers Have Landed,* Adamski claimed that he not only met with an alien but also traveled into space!

By the time he had his contact, Adamski was no stranger to UFOs. He saw his first spaceship on October 9, 1946. He later described the craft as a "large black object similar in shape to a gigantic dirigible." The craft hovered motionlessly. Then it "quickly shot up into space, leaving a fiery trail behind it."

The next year Adamski and four others claimed they saw a fleet of UFOs. He counted 184 of them. Another witness counted 204.

Adamski and a group of friends were convinced that UFOs were real and that humanlike beings piloted them. As proof, they wanted to get good pictures of a craft and to meet its occupants. With this as their goal, Adamski and six of his friends drove into the California desert on November 20, 1952. They were in luck.

As they were eating lunch at a roadside stand, a large cigar-shaped UFO loomed into view. Adamski was sure that the ship had come looking for him. But when he and his friends approached it, the ship disappeared over the nearby mountains. Afraid that it had been frightened away, Adamski asked to be left alone with his cameras.

A flash of light in the sky soon caught his eye. Adamski described it as a small disk-shaped craft sent from the larger "mother ship." He watched as it drifted toward him and settled down about a half-mile away. After he took some pictures, he noticed a manlike creature beckoning to him from some distance away. The man wore sandals and a one-piece suit of shiny brown material. About five feet six inches tall, he had long flowing blond hair, green eyes, and perfect white teeth. His face was tanned. The man looked quite human, even "beautiful," as Adamski later described the creature. Yet Adamski suddenly realized that he was "in the presence of . . . a human being from another world!"

According to Adamski, they managed to communicate by reading each other's minds and by using sign language. Orthon, as the creature was called, said that he was from the planet Venus. He had come to warn about the testing of atomic weapons. Earth had put itself and the solar system in danger through testing. Orthon told Adamski that a number of other Venusians were already living on Earth. Sometimes, Orthon hinted, Earthlings were kidnapped and taken aboard flying saucers.

Orthon showed Adamski his spaceship, which hovered nearby. It was about 35 feet wide and made of a material that sparkled in the light. Despite a warning not to get too close, Adamski accidently moved beneath part of the craft. "My arm was jerked up, and almost at the same instant thrown down against my body," he said. "The force was so strong that, although I could still move the arm, I had no feeling in it as I stepped clear of the ship." It took several weeks for his arm to return to normal.

Before leaving, Orthon asked for a roll of film. He promised to return it soon. With the rest of his film Adamski took pictures of the craft as it rose up and moved off into space.

If Adamski had been the only witness, it is likely that few people would have believed his extraordinary story. But his six friends had watched from a distance. They signed statements about the event. One of them even drew a picture of the Venusian as seen through binoculars.

Then there were the footprints. The soles of Orthon's sandals left marks in the sand that looked like symbols. Were these symbols a message for the world? Adamski took plaster casts of the footprints for further study. Unfortunately, they were never able to interpret the footprints.

The photographs were also a disappointment. The images were too blurry to prove what Adamski had seen.

He had better luck when the spaceship from Venus returned on December 13, 1952. As it swooped down, a porthole opened and Adamski's film was thrown out. A hand waved and the craft zoomed away, but not before Adamski took a number of pictures through a telescope. These clearly showed a saucer with three round objects beneath it, thought to be landing gear. A round cabin with portholes was mounted on top of the ship. These photos were widely published as proof of UFOs.

Why had the film been returned? Adamski found that the original subject had been erased from the film. In its place was what looked like writing. If there was a message, it was never decoded.

These experiences were only the start of George Adamski's fantastic contacts with UFOs. Visitors from space returned many times. They ranged in age from forty to several hundred years. Some were from Mars, others from Saturn. Their mission,

they said, was to warn Earth against destroying itself and other planets. They treated Adamski like an honored guest. Sometimes they took him on trips to other planets. Once he even visited the moon, where he claims he saw cities, mountains, rivers, and lakes. These trips were the basis for Adamski's second book, *Inside the Space Ships*, published in 1955.

George Adamski became quite a celebrity. He appeared frequently on radio and TV. Many people thought he was crazy or an outrageous fraud. Others were convinced he was telling the truth. Today we know that a number of Adamski's claims are false. They could never have happened. No human could possibly survive on Venus. And since 1969, several landings on the moon by astronauts have proved that it has no cities or earthlike scenery. As for Adamski's pictures of UFOs, many of those have been discovered to be fakes, and many others have been called into question.

Not everyone feels that all of Adamski's claims have been disproved, though. Here is how he describes what he saw from a porthole on one of his space trips in the early 50s. "I was amazed to see that the background of space is totally dark. Yet there were manifestations taking place all around us, as though billions upon billions of fireflies were flickering everywhere, moving in all directions, as fireflies do.

However, these were of many colors, a . . . fireworks display that was beautiful to the point of being awesome."

Here is how astronaut John Glenn described his view during the first United States orbit of Earth in 1962. "The spacecraft was surrounded by luminous particles. These particles were a light yellowish green color. It was as if the spacecraft were moving through a field of fireflies."

Did George Adamski engineer a fabulous hoax to achieve fame and fortune? He firmly denied it. "Surface thinkers might like to conclude that I had had a very original dream. Or that I may be out to make money for myself in the field of science fiction. I can assure such persons that nothing is farther from the truth." ■

*If you have been timed while reading this selection, enter your reading time below. Then turn to the Words-per-Minute table on page 154 and look up your reading speed (words per minute). Enter your reading speed on the graph on page 156.*

READING TIME: Unit 2

———— : ————

*Minutes*      *Seconds*

# How well did you read?

- *Answer the four types of questions that follow. The directions for each type of question tell you how to mark your answers.*

- *When you have finished all four exercises, check your work by using the answer key on page 150. For each right answer, put a check mark (✓) on the line beside the box. For each wrong answer, write the correct answer on the line.*

- *For scoring each exercise, follow the directions below the questions.*

## A  FINDING THE MAIN IDEA

Look at the three statements below. One expresses the main idea of the story you just read. A good main idea statement answers two questions: it tells *who* or *what* is the subject of the story, and it answers the understood question *does what?* or *is what?* Another statement is *too broad;* it is vague and doesn't tell much about the topic of the story. The third statement is *too narrow;* it tells about only one part of the story.

Match the statements with the three answer choices below by writing the letter of each answer in the box in front of the statement it goes with.

**M—Main Idea      B—Too Broad      N—Too Narrow**

____ ☐ 1. George Adamski was convinced that he met Orthon, an alien from the planet Venus, in 1952.

____ ☐ 2. By the 1950s many people believed that aliens from other planets regularly visited Earth.

____ ☐ 3. George Adamski claimed that he talked with aliens from outer space'and had traveled to other planets.

____ Score 15 points for a correct *M* answer

____ Score 5 points for each correct *B* or *N* answer

____ TOTAL SCORE: Finding the Main Idea

## B  RECALLING FACTS

How well do you remember the facts in the story you just read? Put an *x* in the box in front of the correct answer to each of the multiple-choice questions below.

1. George Adamski claimed that he saw his first spaceship in
____ ☐ a. 1946.
____ ☐ b. 1952.
____ ☐ c. 1962.

2. The first alien from outer space George Adamski saw was wearing
____ ☐ a. clothes that sparkled.
____ ☐ b. a space suit, helmets, and boots.
____ ☐ c. a shiny brown one-piece suit and sandals.

3. The aliens George Adamski met came to Earth to
____ ☐ a. take back information to Venus.
____ ☐ b. warn about the effects of atomic testing.
____ ☐ c. start a new colony.

4. The aliens George Adamski saw came from
____ ☐ a. several different planets.
____ ☐ b. the same planet, Venus.
____ ☐ c. Venus and Saturn only.

5. When people disputed the truth of George Adamski's claims, he
____ ☐ a. admitted they were false.
____ ☐ b. refused to answer.
____ ☐ c. maintained he was telling the truth.

Score 5 points for each correct answer

____ TOTAL SCORE: Recalling Facts

## C  MAKING INFERENCES

An inference is a judgment that is made or an idea that is arrived at based on facts or on information that is given. You make an inference when you understand something that is *not* stated directly but that is *implied*, or suggested, by the facts that are given.

Below are five statements that are judgments or ideas that have been arrived at from the facts of the story. Write the letter *C* in the box in front of each statement that is a correct inference. Write the letter *F* in front of each faulty inference.

**C—Correct Inference      F—Faulty Inference**

____ ☐ 1. There was an increase in UFO stories during the 1950s.

____ ☐ 2. George Adamski was an unusual person.

____ ☐ 3. Orthon was worried about the Earth and the solar system.

____ ☐ 4. John Glenn's description of space proves that George Adamski was telling the truth.

____ ☐ 5. George Adamski was most likely a fraud and his stories a hoax.

Score 5 points for each correct answer

____ TOTAL SCORE: Making Inferences

## D USING WORDS PRECISELY

Each of the numbered sentences below contains an underlined word or phrase from the story you have just read. Under the sentence are three definitions. One is a *synonym*, a word that means the same or almost the same thing: *big* and *large*. One is an *antonym*, a word that has the opposite or nearly opposite meaning: *love* and *hate*. One is an unrelated word; it has a completely *different* meaning. Match the definitions with the three answer choices by writing the letter that stands for each answer in the box in front of the definition it goes with.

**S—Synonym     A—Antonym     D—Different**

1. But the claims of 61-year-old George Adamski <u>ushered in</u> a new era.

____ ☐ a. introduce; brought on the scene

____ ☐ b. escorted to a seat

____ ☐ c. ended; closed out

2. <u>Despite</u> a warning not to get too close, Adamski accidently moved beneath part of the craft.

____ ☐ a. concerned; careful

____ ☐ b. in spite of; regardless

____ ☐ c. disliked

3. Many people thought he was crazy or an <u>outrageous</u> fraud.

____ ☐ a. disappointed

____ ☐ b. ordinary

____ ☐ c. shocking

4. "The spacecraft was surrounded by <u>luminous</u> particles."

____ ☐ a. glowing light

____ ☐ b. dark

____ ☐ c. colorful

5. Did George Adamski engineer a fabulous <u>hoax</u> to achieve fame and fortune?

____ ☐ a. truthfulness

____ ☐ b. plan; idea

____ ☐ c. trick; joke

____ Score 3 points for each correct *S* answer
____ Score 1 point for each correct *A* or *D* answer

____ TOTAL SCORE: Using Words Precisely

● *Enter the four total scores in the spaces below, and add them together to find your Critical Reading Score. Then record your Critical Reading Score on the graph on page 157.*

| | |
|---|---|
| _____ | Finding the Main Idea |
| _____ | Recalling Facts |
| _____ | Making Inferences |
| _____ | Using Words Precisely |
| _____ | CRITICAL READING SCORE: Unit 2 |

Outside an isolated farmhouse in Kelly, Kentucky, short creatures with big bald heads and shining yellow eyes scurried about. Elmer "Lucky" Sutton and Billy Ray Taylor decided to shoot first and ask questions later. But their firepower didn't kill the intruders or even draw blood. The Kelly-Hopkinsville siege was a classic example of a close encounter of the third kind.

# The Kelly-Hopkinsville Siege

Like people on Earth, creatures from outer space are reported to come in all shapes and sizes. Some are tall and look almost human. Others are short with large round bald heads and strange slanted eyes. But the strangest aliens of all were seen in 1955 in the small town of Kelly, Kentucky.

On August 21 the five members of the Sutton family were enjoying dinner with friends. Glenie Langford and her three children were there, along with Billy Ray Taylor and his wife, June. As it grew dark, 21-year-old Billy Ray went outside for a drink of water at the well. A moment later he was back, so excited he could barely speak.

"You'll never believe what I saw!" he sputtered.

"Why don't you try us?" drawled Elmer "Lucky" Sutton, chuckling at his friend.

"It was a UFO, real bright, with an exhaust all the colors of the rainbow!" Billy Ray exclaimed. "It flew right over my head. Then it landed in that gully right next to the house!"

No one at the table took Billy Ray's story seriously. They all agreed that what he had seen had probably been a shooting star.

About an hour later the Sutton dog started barking wildly. When Lucky and Billy Ray went to the door, they nearly fainted from fright. Walking slowly toward them was a small glowing figure. Its arms were raised.

Huge, radiant yellow eyes stared from the sides of a large, round head. Its mouth was a slit stretching across its face, and its ears were like an elephant's. It had claws for hands.

Not waiting to ask questions, the two men grabbed their guns—a 20-gauge shotgun and a .22-caliber rifle. When the creature came within 20 feet of the house, they opened fire. The creature did a backward somersault and disappeared into the night.

For a moment, all was quiet. Then a scratching sound on the roof sent the two men outside. Another creature was on top of the house! Firing again, the men watched in disbelief as the creature floated to the ground and trotted off on all fours. Lucky's bullets had hit their mark, but they sounded as if they had struck metal!

The families huddled inside behind locked doors. Through the windows they could see the creatures still wandering outside, although now they seemed afraid to come too close. What would happen next? After three hours of terror, the families decided to make a run for it. At about 11:00 P.M. they dashed for their cars and sped toward the police station in nearby Hopkinsville.

With 11 witnesses telling the same story, Chief Russell Greenwell wasted no time. Taking Deputy George Batts, Sergeant Pritchett, three other officers, and a local reporter, he followed the Suttons and

their friends back to the farm.

On the way they saw two streaks of light and heard a loud banging sound. But when they reached the farm only a glowing patch on the ground where an alien had landed and a few bullet holes suggested that anything unusual had happened. Still the chief was impressed. "Something frightened these people, something beyond their comprehension," he said. He agreed to come back at daylight to search further.

Still shaken, the family went to bed. If they slept at all, it was not for long. At 2:30 in the morning the creatures were back, staring into the farmhouse windows with their huge yellow eyes. Once again the men shot at the creatures, with no better luck than before. But by 5:00 A.M. the creatures had gone. It was the last time the Suttons saw them.

The nightmare seemed over. But now the Suttons endured a different kind of siege. Reporters from all over the state appeared at the farmhouse. The Suttons gave endless interviews. Police and UFO investigators combed the grounds for clues. When nothing was found, the Suttons were accused of lying. They were called religious fanatics. But they stuck to their story. They swore they were telling the truth.

The Suttons and their friends never tried to make money from what happened. And after the brief flurry of excitement, life in Kelly went on much as it always had—uneventful.

So far no one has come up with a logical explanation for what happened on the Sutton farm. One idea—that the creatures were monkeys that had escaped from a traveling circus—seemed too silly to be taken seriously. Monkeys jump; they don't float to the ground! And there hadn't been any circuses in or near town. If the creatures were from another world, what were their intentions? They never tried to harm anyone. Perhaps the raised arms of the first creature to approach the house were a sign that they meant no harm.

Whatever the explanation, what came to be called the Kelly-Hopkinsville siege is a UFO classic. Researchers call it a close encounter of the third kind: a close-range sighting of a UFO and its occupants. What makes it special is the number of witnesses. Eight adults and three children insist that what happened was real. No one has been able to explain exactly what occurred that August evening. ∎

*If you have been timed while reading this selection, enter your reading time below. Then turn to the Words-per-Minute table on page 154 and look up your reading speed (words per minute). Enter your reading speed on the graph on page 156.*

READING TIME: Unit 3

_____ : _____
*Minutes        Seconds*

# How well did you read?

- *Answer the four types of questions that follow. The directions for each type of question tell you how to mark your answers.*

- *When you have finished all four exercises, check your work by using the answer key on page 150. For each right answer, put a check mark (✓) on the line beside the box. For each wrong answer, write the correct answer on the line.*

- *For scoring each exercise, follow the directions below the questions.*

## A  FINDING THE MAIN IDEA

Look at the three statements below. One expresses the main idea of the story you just read. A good main idea statement answers two questions: it tells *who* or *what* is the subject of the story, and it answers the understood question *does what?* or *is what?* Another statement is *too broad;* it is vague and doesn't tell much about the topic of the story. The third statement is *too narrow;* it tells about only one part of the story.

Match the statements with the three answer choices below by writing the letter of each answer in the box in front of the statement it goes with.

**M—Main Idea**      **B—Too Broad**      **N—Too Narrow**

_____ ☐ 1. On the evening of August 21, 1955, 11 people from Kelly, Kentucky, said they met with aliens.

_____ ☐ 2. No one has been able to prove or disprove the story of 11 people from Kelly, Kentucky, who claim they had seen aliens.

_____ ☐ 3. The Kelly-Hopkinsville siege is considered by many to be a UFO classic encounter.

_____ Score 15 points for a correct *M* answer

_____ Score 5 points for each correct *B* or *N* answer

**_____** TOTAL SCORE: Finding the Main Idea

## B  RECALLING FACTS

How well do you remember the facts in the story you just read? Put an *x* in the box in front of the correct answer to each of the multiple-choice questions below.

1. Billy Ray Taylor first met the aliens
   - ___ ☐ a. while he was getting water from a well.
   - ___ ☐ b. at a picnic with his wife.
   - ___ ☐ c. driving from Kelly to Hopkinsville.

2. Billy Ray's wife and friends thought he
   - ___ ☐ a. was playing a joke on them.
   - ___ ☐ b. was telling the truth.
   - ___ ☐ c. had seen a shooting star.

3. After a few scary hours, the families agreed to
   - ___ ☐ a. surrender to the aliens.
   - ___ ☐ b. try to kill the aliens.
   - ___ ☐ c. drive to the police station.

4. After the families told their story to the police chief, he
   - ___ ☐ a. laughed in disbelief.
   - ___ ☐ b. asked for proof and other witnesses.
   - ___ ☐ c. agreed that something had frightened them.

5. When the police searched the farm, the only sign that something strange had occurred was a
   - ___ ☐ a. part of the alien spacecraft.
   - ___ ☐ b. glowing patch on the ground.
   - ___ ☐ c. strange message left by the aliens.

Score 5 points for each correct answer

___ TOTAL SCORE: Recalling Facts

## C  MAKING INFERENCES

An inference is a judgment that is made or an idea that is arrived at based on facts or on information that is given. You make an inference when you understand something that is *not* stated directly but that is *implied*, or suggested, by the facts that are given.

Below are five statements that are judgments or ideas that have been arrived at from the facts of the story. Write the letter *C* in the box in front of each statement that is a correct inference. Write the letter *F* in front of each faulty inference.

**C—Correct Inference      F—Faulty Inference**

- ___ ☐ 1. Billy Ray Taylor always played practical jokes on his family.
- ___ ☐ 2. The alien creatures were hostile toward Billy Ray and his friends.
- ___ ☐ 3. Police Chief Russell could tell that the families were upset.
- ___ ☐ 4. The aliens were determined creatures.
- ___ ☐ 5. The aliens that the two families saw were probably monkeys.

Score 5 points for each correct answer

___ TOTAL SCORE: Making Inferences

## D USING WORDS PRECISELY

Each of the numbered sentences below contains an underlined word or phrase from the story you have just read. Under the sentence are three definitions. One is a *synonym*, a word that means the same or almost the same thing: *big* and *large*. One is an *antonym*, a word that has the opposite or nearly opposite meaning: *love* and *hate*. One is an unrelated word; it has a completely *different* meaning. Match the definitions with the three answer choices by writing the letter that stands for each answer in the box in front of the definition it goes with.

**S—Synonym     A—Antonym     D—Different**

1. "Why don't you try us?" <u>drawled</u> Elmer "Lucky" Sutton, chuckling at his friend.

   ____ ☐ a. spoke slowly

   ____ ☐ b. called out

   ____ ☐ c. talked rapidly

2. "Something frightened these people, something beyond their <u>comprehension</u>," he [the police chief] said.

   ____ ☐ a. misunderstanding

   ____ ☐ b. understanding

   ____ ☐ c. appreciation

3. But now the Suttons endured a different kind of <u>siege</u>.

   ____ ☐ a. public attention

   ____ ☐ b. attack

   ____ ☐ c. retreat

4. And after the brief <u>flurry</u> of excitement, life in Kelly went on much as it always had—uneventful.

   ____ ☐ a. stillness

   ____ ☐ b. storm

   ____ ☐ c. confusion

5. So far no one has come up with a <u>logical</u> explanation for what happened on the Sutton farm.

   ____ ☐ a. thought out

   ____ ☐ b. unreasonable

   ____ ☐ c. senseless

____ Score 3 points for each correct *S* answer
____ Score 1 point for each correct *A* or *D* answer

____ TOTAL SCORE: Using Words Precisely

● *Enter the four total scores in the spaces below, and add them together to find your Critical Reading Score. Then record your Critical Reading Score on the graph on page 157.*

_____ Finding the Main Idea
_____ Recalling Facts
_____ Making Inferences
_____ Using Words Precisely

_____ CRITICAL READING SCORE: Unit 3

*For two nights in a row, Reverend William Booth Gill had something very interesting to write in his diary. He had seen UFOs! The spaceships hovered over his mission on the island of New Guinea just after sunset each day. Gill witnessed the amazing sight with his followers. After the second sighting, Gill wrote in his diary: "7:45. Evensong [evening prayer] over and sky covered with cloud. Visibility very poor. No UFOs in sight."*

# An Encounter in New Guinea

What has been called one of the great classics in UFO history happened on the other side of the world. The year was 1959. The place was a remote religious mission on the tropical island of New Guinea, which is located in the Pacific Ocean, north of Australia.

Around 6:45 P.M. on June 26, Reverend William Booth Gill stepped outside the mission to study the evening sky. He found Venus, the brightest star. But what was that very bright, sparkling object above it? Reverend Gill stared as the sparkling object seemed to descend. It was heading straight for the mission!

Two of the mission's staff came running at his excited call. Yes, they saw it too. Soon other people from the mission were gazing at the astonishing sight.

As it got closer the viewers could see that the object resembled a huge disk with a wide base. There was an upper deck with what looked like legs. Portholes were visible around the side. While the large disk hovered about 300 feet from the ground, small UFOs flew around it. From time to time blue beams shot into the sky.

After watching for about 15 minutes, Reverend Gill thought he noticed movement inside the disk. He was right. Through the portholes four humanlike figures were visible. The figures seemed to glow.

The surprised group stood by quietly, transfixed for about four hours. Then about 11:00 P.M. the disk zoomed away.

Having read about UFOs, Reverend Gill was convinced that he had seen a "mother ship"—a large spacecraft used as a station for other smaller craft. He was equally sure that he had seen aliens inside. Would they return? Gill did not have to wait long for the answer.

The next evening the spacecraft was back. It was shortly after sunset, but Gill could see the object quite clearly. Once again he could make out four figures on what seemed to be a deck on top of the huge disk. "There is no doubt that they were human," he said. While one of the figures seemed to be operating equipment, two others near the center of the deck were bending over and raising their arms. One of them appeared to be looking down at the men on the ground.

Acting on impulse, Gill decided to wave a greeting. To his surprise the figure waved back! When the others on the ground waved their arms over their heads, the figures on the UFO did the same! As a further test, Gill tried signalling the craft with a flashlight. After one or two flashes, the disk "wavered back and forth like a pendulum." Said Reverend Gill, "There seemed to be no doubt that our movements were answered."

After awhile the figures on the UFO

seemed to tire of the game and disappeared below deck. But at 6:25 P.M. they reappeared. Under a blue spotlight the figures worked on something for five minutes or so. Then Gill made a very strange decision. He and his staff ignored the UFO while they went inside to eat dinner! Half an hour later they returned outside. But by then the UFO had moved some distance away. Finally it disappeared from sight.

If you had a chance to meet visitors from outer space, would you wave to them and then go to dinner? That does not seem very likely. Yet that is exactly what Reverend Gill claims he did.

Doubting Gill's story, the Australian Department of Air suggested that the sightings "most probably . . . were reflections on a cloud of a major light source of unknown origin." The Royal Australian Air Force offered another logical explanation. Based on "an analysis of bearings and angles above the horizon," the RAAF concluded that "at least three of the lights were planets, perhaps Jupiter, Saturn, and Mars." Neither of these theories is given much credit.

As unlikely as his story may be, many who talked with Reverend Gill at the time of the event believed he was telling the truth. And in 1977, 18 years later, he still stood by his story. But why did he choose to have dinner in the midst of one of the most spectacular

UFO sightings in history? "We were a bit fed up that they wouldn't come down after all the waving," he explained in a 1977 interview. "This is the difficult thing to get across to people. Here was a flying saucer. Therefore, it must have been a traumatic experience. It was nothing of the kind."

Many UFO investigators find it difficult to believe that Reverend Gill, a well-educated priest, would make up such a fantastic story just as a hoax. Also in his favor are the 37 other people at the mission who claimed that they too saw the objects in the sky. It is hard to argue with that many witnesses. ■

*If you have been timed while reading this selection, enter your reading time below. Then turn to the Words-per-Minute table on page 154 and look up your reading speed (words per minute). Enter your reading speed on the graph on page 156.*

| READING TIME: Unit 4 |
| :--- |
| _____ : _____ |
| *Minutes*     *Seconds* |

# How well did you read?

- *Answer the four types of questions that follow. The directions for each type of question tell you how to mark your answers.*

- *When you have finished all four exercises, check your work by using the answer key on page 150. For each right answer, put a check mark (✓) on the line beside the box. For each wrong answer, write the correct answer on the line.*

- *For scoring each exercise, follow the directions below the questions.*

using the answer key on page 150.

## A   FINDING THE MAIN IDEA

Look at the three statements below. One expresses the main idea of the story you just read. A good main idea statement answers two questions: it tells *who* or *what* is the subject of the story, and it answers the understood question *does what?* or *is what?* Another statement is *too broad;* it is vague and doesn't tell much about the topic of the story. The third statement is *too narrow;* it tells about only one part of the story.

Match the statements with the three answer choices below by writing the letter of each answer in the box in front of the statement it goes with.

**M—Main Idea**     **B—Too Broad**     **N—Too Narrow**

_____ ☐ 1. Experts cannot prove that Reverend Gill actually saw UFOs, but many people believe Gill and the other eyewitnesses.

_____ ☐ 2. Reverend William Booth Gill reported seeing UFOs and aliens in New Guinea in June 1959.

_____ ☐ 3. UFOs have been reported in many areas of the world and in areas as remote as New Guinea.

_____ Score 15 points for a correct *M* answer

_____ Score 5 points for each correct *B* or *N* answer

_____ TOTAL SCORE: Finding the Main Idea

## B RECALLING FACTS

How well do you remember the facts in the story you just read?
Put an *x* in the box in front of the correct answer to each of the
multiple-choice questions below.

1. New Guinea is an island near
   ____ ☐ a. Africa.
   ____ ☐ b. South America.
   ____ ☐ c. Australia.

2. Reverend Gill was in New Guinea
   ____ ☐ a. running a religious mission.
   ____ ☐ b. taking a short vacation.
   ____ ☐ c. investigating reports of UFO sightings.

3. When Reverend Gill waved at the creatures in the UFO, they
   ____ ☐ a. landed nearby.
   ____ ☐ b. waved back.
   ____ ☐ c. sped away in fear.

4. Reverend Gill thought the creatures in the UFO were
   ____ ☐ a. human.
   ____ ☐ b. nonhuman.
   ____ ☐ c. robots.

5. During the second sighting of the UFO, Reverend Gill
   and his followers
   ____ ☐ a. tried to shoot it down.
   ____ ☐ b. left it to eat dinner.
   ____ ☐ c. pleaded with the occupants to go away.

Score 5 points for each correct answer

____ TOTAL SCORE: Recalling Facts

## C MAKING INFERENCES

An inference is a judgment that is made or an idea that is arrived
at based on facts or on information that is given. You make an
inference when you understand something that is *not* stated
directly but that is *implied,* or suggested, by the facts that are given.

Below are five statements that are judgments or ideas that have
been arrived at from the facts of the story. Write the letter *C* in
the box in front of each statement that is a correct inference. Write
the letter *F* in front of each faulty inference.

**C—Correct Inference     F—Faulty Inference**

____ ☐ 1. Some UFO investigators believe Reverend Gill
         and the other eyewitnesses.

____ ☐ 2. The Australian Department of Air believed in
         the UFO sighting.

____ ☐ 3. Reverend Gill occasionally acted without thinking.

____ ☐ 4. Reverend Gill neglected his duties at the mission.

☐ 5. Reverend Gill had no interest in UFOs or aliens.

Score 5 points for each correct answer

____ TOTAL SCORE: Making Inferences

## D USING WORDS PRECISELY

Each of the numbered sentences below contains an underlined word or phrase from the story you have just read. Under the sentence are three definitions. One is a *synonym,* a word that means the same or almost the same thing: *big* and *large.* One is an *antonym,* a word that has the opposite or nearly opposite meaning: *love* and *hate.* One is an unrelated word; it has a completely *different* meaning. Match the definitions with the three answer choices by writing the letter that stands for each answer in the box in front of the definition it goes with.

**S—Synonym        A—Antonym        D—Different**

1. The place was a <u>remote</u> religious mission on the tropical island of New Guinea, which is located in the Pacific Ocean, north of Australia.

____ ☐ a. out-of-the-way

____ ☐ b. far away

____ ☐ c. nearby

2. The surprised group stood by quietly, <u>transfixed</u> for about four hours.

____ ☐ a. stunned

____ ☐ b. moved back and forth

____ ☐ c. held motionless

3. Acting on <u>impulse</u>, Gill decided to wave a greeting.

____ ☐ a. carefully thought out

____ ☐ b. sudden decision to act

____ ☐ c. bold action

4. Neither of these <u>theories</u> is given much credit.

____ ☐ a. guesses

____ ☐ b. ideas or beliefs

____ ☐ c. proven laws

5. "Therefore, it [seeing a flying saucer] must have been a <u>traumatic</u> experience."

____ ☐ a. stressful

____ ☐ b. pleasant

____ ☐ c. harmful

____ Score 3 points for each correct *S* answer

____ Score 1 point for each correct *A* or *D* answer

____ TOTAL SCORE: Using Words Precisely

● *Enter the four total scores in the spaces below, and add them together to find your Critical Reading Score. Then record your Critical Reading Score on the graph on page 157.*

| | |
|---|---|
| _____ | Finding the Main Idea |
| _____ | Recalling Facts |
| _____ | Making Inferences |
| _____ | Using Words Precisely |
| _____ | CRITICAL READING SCORE:  Unit 4 |

When George asked to go fishing at Richard's Bay, his friend Edwin agreed to take him. Edwin was in for a big surprise. George would be ending his stay on Earth! It would be the last time Edwin would see his good friend, but not the last time he would hear from him. . . .

# Aliens on Earth?

"Hey Ed, I think I've got a big one!" George shouted as he began to reel in his line. About 10 yards away, a silvery tail slapped the water, confirming George's catch.

"Must be a whale," agreed Edwin, watching George's fishing rod bend almost in half. "Don't let it get away!"

Grunting with the exertion, George slowly reeled in his prize. "What a fighter! This baby's going to make a feast!" he exclaimed proudly.

Eighteen-year-old Edwin ran to the shore and reached out to grab the line. "Biggest fish I've ever seen," said Edwin, hauling the flopping fish onto shore.

George removed the hook with a deft motion. He squinted at the catch with a practiced eye. "It's at least 30 pounds," he announced, removing his knife from his pocket. "I'm going to fillet it here. The less weight we have to carry, the better."

"I don't blame you," said Edwin. "That black bag of yours weighs a ton."

George looked at Edwin and smiled. "You've been wondering about that bag I brought along, haven't you?"

"I am curious," Edwin admitted sheepishly. "You never brought it with you when we went fishing before."

"Well, tonight's your lucky night, son. You've been curious about the lights we've been seeing out here. Now I'm going to give you absolute proof that spaceships exist!" With a flourish, George untied the mysterious black bag and removed some sort of unusual device.

"What's that?" asked Edwin.

"This is a radio receiver. Listen."

When George switched on the receiver they heard garbled speech. Then Edwin heard a strange language. He looked questioningly at his friend.

"Wait," said George.

As the minutes dragged on Edwin began to wonder if the whole thing was a joke. After all, he didn't really know George all that well. It had been only a few months before that George had taken the post of supervisor at the factory in Durban, South Africa, where Edwin worked as a radio mechanic. Despite the fact that George was almost old enough to be his father, the two got along very well. Their friendship grew on their frequent fishing trips to Patterson's Groyne. Still, George was a quiet man who didn't talk much about his personal life.

Suddenly George pointed to a light in the sky about the size of a tennis ball. "That's a spacecraft zeroing in on us," he announced.

To Edwin's amazement, an English voice began speaking over the radio. "I am Wy-Ora, captain of the spaceship," said the voice. "We come from the planet Koldas."

The voice explained that one of the crew, named Valdar, was actually George. George's job was to find people on Earth to spread the word about their mission.

According to Edwin, George then gave instructions over the radio to the craft. In response to his orders, the craft performed various maneuvers. Edwin was impressed.

In the weeks that followed George continued to impress Edwin. "I'm not the only alien here on Earth," George explained. "There are hundreds of us." Once when he thought no one was looking, George physically moved a machine that had taken a crane and five people to set into place.

One day George quit his job and asked Edwin to take him fishing at Richard's Bay. "It's time for me to leave," George announced. "But don't worry, friend, I'll keep in touch." Edwin watched as George changed into a one-piece uniform. Then, handing Edwin the radio, he told him what to do.

Following George's instructions Edwin knelt behind a sand dune. In a few minutes a light appeared in the sky. As it grew nearer, Edwin made out a disk-shaped flying saucer, about 150 feet wide. On top of the disk was a dome, inside of which Edwin could see a figure. The craft zoomed up to the beach and landed, settling only long enough for George to board. In seconds it took off and disappeared.

True to his word, George has kept in touch with his friend Edwin. Since those fishing trips with George in 1960, Edwin has become quite a celebrity and has a number of followers. He claims that he receives frequent messages from his old boss. Some broadcasts describe the way of life on the planet Koldas. Others describe the aliens' purpose on Earth. According to George, rival groups are trying to control the Earth. Edwin has also been given technical information about the aliens' spacecraft.

Is Edwin telling the truth? No one has ever been able to prove absolutely that people have had contact with aliens. Edwin's entire story could be a fake, but it would have been an expensive one. Cynthia Hind, a UFO investigator, decided to find out. She listened to a broadcast and examined the radio receiver. But Hind had no experience with radio equipment and was unable to comment on its workings. She did say that listening to the broadcast had a "disturbing effect on me."

Edwin's followers, however, firmly believe that the broadcasts are real. ■

*If you have been timed while reading this selection, enter your reading time below. Then turn to the Words-per-Minute table on page 154 and look up your reading speed (words per minute). Enter your reading speed on the graph on page 156.*

READING TIME: Unit 5

_____ : _____
*Minutes          Seconds*

# How well did you read?

- *Answer the four types of questions that follow. The directions for each type of question tell you how to mark your answers.*

- *When you have finished all four exercises, check your work by using the answer key on page 150. For each right answer, put a check mark (✓) on the line beside the box. For each wrong answer, write the correct answer on the line.*

- *For scoring each exercise, follow the directions below the questions.*

using the answer key on page 150.

## A FINDING THE MAIN IDEA

Look at the three statements below. One expresses the main idea of the story you just read. A good main idea statement answers two questions: it tells *who* or *what* is the subject of the story, and it answers the understood question *does what?* or *is what?* Another statement is *too broad;* it is vague and doesn't tell much about the topic of the story. The third statement is *too narrow;* it tells about only one part of the story.

Match the statements with the three answer choices below by writing the letter of each answer in the box in front of the statement it goes with.

**M—Main Idea     B—Too Broad     N—Too Narrow**

_____ ☐ 1. Claims that people have had contact with aliens have never been proven.

_____ ☐ 2. Cynthia Hind was the UFO investigator who listened to the aliens' broadcast.

_____ ☐ 3. Although the story is unproven, Edwin claims that his friend George is really an alien from the planet Koldas.

_____ Score 15 points for a correct *M* answer

_____ Score 5 points for each correct *B* or *N* answer

**_____ TOTAL SCORE: Finding the Main Idea**

## B RECALLING FACTS

How well do you remember the facts in the story you just read? Put an *x* in the box in front of the correct answer to each of the multiple-choice questions below.

1. George and Edwin
   - ____ ☐ a. were friends.
   - ____ ☐ b. disliked each other.
   - ____ ☐ c. distrusted each other.

2. George and Edwin worked at a factory in
   - ____ ☐ a. South America.
   - ____ ☐ b. South Africa.
   - ____ ☐ c. the United States.

3. George was
   - ____ ☐ a. younger than Edwin.
   - ____ ☐ b. about the same age as Edwin.
   - ____ ☐ c. much older than Edwin.

4. Wy-Ora told Edwin that
   - ____ ☐ a. the aliens wanted to live on Earth.
   - ____ ☐ b. Edwin wouldn't remember the broadcast.
   - ____ ☐ c. George was really an alien named Valdar.

5. When George went away, Edwin
   - ____ ☐ a. forgot about him.
   - ____ ☐ b. kept in touch with his friend.
   - ____ ☐ c. never talked about George again.

Score 5 points for each correct answer

____ TOTAL SCORE: Recalling Facts

## C MAKING INFERENCES

An inference is a judgment that is made or an idea that is arrived at based on facts or on information that is given. You make an inference when you understand something that is *not* stated directly but that is *implied,* or suggested, by the facts that are given.

Below are five statements that are judgments or ideas that have been arrived at from the facts of the story. Write the letter *C* in the box in front of each statement that is a correct inference. Write the letter *F* in front of each faulty inference.

**C—Correct Inference      F—Faulty Inference**

____ ☐ 1. George and Edwin enjoyed each other's company.

____ ☐ 2. The aliens were concerned that Edwin knew about them.

____ ☐ 3. Cynthia Hind could not say whether or not the broadcasts were real.

____ ☐ 4. Edwin was relieved when George went away.

____ ☐ 5. Edwin believed everything that George told him.

Score 5 points for each correct answer

____ TOTAL SCORE: Making Inferences

## D USING WORDS PRECISELY

Each of the numbered sentences below contains an underlined word or phrase from the story you have just read. Under the sentence are three definitions. One is a *synonym,* a word that means the same or almost the same thing: *big* and *large.* One is an *antonym,* a word that has the opposite or nearly opposite meaning: *love* and *hate.* One is an unrelated word; it has a completely *different* meaning. Match the definitions with the three answer choices by writing the letter that stands for each answer in the box in front of the definition it goes with.

**S—Synonym     A—Antonym     D—Different**

1. George removed the hook with a <u>deft</u> motion.

____ ☐ a. skillful

____ ☐ b. quick

____ ☐ c. awkward

2. "I am curious," Edwin admitted <u>sheepishly.</u>

____ ☐ a. boldly

____ ☐ b. with shame

____ ☐ c. bashfully

3. "Now I'm going to give you <u>absolute</u> proof that spaceships exist!"

____ ☐ a. certain

____ ☐ b. limited

____ ☐ c. basic

4. With a <u>flourish</u>, George untied the mysterious black bag and removed some sort of device.

____ ☐ a. wave

____ ☐ b. showy movement

____ ☐ c. fearful move

5. When George switched on the receiver they heard <u>garbled</u> speech.

____ ☐ a. troubled

____ ☐ b. clear; to the point

____ ☐ c. scrambled; mixed-up

____ Score 3 points for each correct *S* answer
____ Score 1 point for each correct *A* or *D* answer

____ TOTAL SCORE: Using Words Precisely

● *Enter the four total scores in the spaces below, and add them together to find your Critical Reading Score. Then record your Critical Reading Score on the graph on page 157.*

| | |
|---|---|
| _____ | Finding the Main Idea |
| _____ | Recalling Facts |
| _____ | Making Inferences |
| _____ | Using Words Precisely |
| _____ | CRITICAL READING SCORE: Unit 5 |

*Highway Patrol officer Lonnie Zamora may have wished he never turned onto that gravel road outside Socorro, New Mexico. That's where he saw an egg-shaped object with a bluish flame underneath slowly rise from the desert floor. When state trooper M. S. Chavez arrived at the scene, he and Zamora discovered burning brush and an indentation where the craft had apparently taken off.*

# The Socorro Sighting

It was 5:45 in the evening on April 24, 1964. Deputy Marshal Lonnie Zamora of Socorro, New Mexico, had put in a long day. He was looking forward to a good dinner. But all thoughts of food disappeared when a speeding car suddenly shot past him. Pressing down on the accelerator, Zamora gave chase. As they reached the outskirts of town the speeder seemed to go even faster. Zamora felt his adrenalin pumping. He pressed harder on the pedal.

Suddenly Zamora heard a loud roar. A flame of blue-orange light briefly lit the sky. Was something on fire? Zamora knew that dynamite was stored in a nearby shack. A fire there could mean big trouble. Reluctantly, he stopped the chase to investigate. Turning onto a side road, the policeman headed for the shack.

Something shiny glinted in the fading sun. Could it be an overturned car? As he got closer, Zamora saw two people standing next to the vehicle. One of them "seemed to turn and look straight at my car and seemed startled—seemed to jump somewhat," he recalled. Still, they appeared fairly normal, like "small adults or large kids." Both were wearing white coveralls. Zamora radioed the sheriff's office that he was going to investigate an accident.

About 100 feet from the crash, Zamora stopped his car and got out. The vehicle no longer resembled a car. It was white and shaped like an egg. The egg was perched on four legs. No doors or windows were visible. Before he could get any closer, Zamora heard a strange roaring sound. Frightened, he raced back to his car, knocking off his glasses. Taking cover, he watched as the shiny vehicle began to rise over the blue-orange flame. "It appeared to go in [a] straight line and at [the] same height— possibly 10 to 15 feet from the ground, and it cleared the dynamite shack by about three feet! . . . Object was traveling very fast. It seemed to rise up, and take off immediately across country." Without his glasses, Zamora couldn't see very well. But he did notice some kind of red lettering on the side of the craft.

Once the craft disappeared, Zamora felt a little better. Finding his glasses, he got back on the radio. "Can you see it?" he excitedly asked the dispatcher. The answer was "no."

Zamora was still shaking when New Mexico state trooper M. S. Chavez arrived a short while later. "You look like you've seen a ghost," said Chavez.

"I feel like I have," answered Zamora.

Zamora pointed to where the craft had been. Brush was still burning. Both men saw large and small indentations in the ground. In a few minutes, investigators crowded the scene. They documented the burn marks and measured four squarish imprints in the sand. They examined smaller marks nearby that could have been footprints or perhaps dents made by a ladder used to board the craft.

Anyone who knew Lonnie Zamora did not doubt his story. He was not the kind of person to tell lies. He was a well-respected police officer. However, Zamora's story had one major flaw: He was the only person to see the craft and its occupants. There were reports of people who had seen a blue flame in the area. Someone had seen the police car drive toward the site. A man who worked in a gas station close by said that a tourist had come to his station on April 24—the same day as the sighting. Just before Lonnie Zamora's encounter, the tourist said he had seen a silver craft floating in the air. Unfortunately, the man never came forward with his story.

Scores of investigators spoke with Lonnie Zamora. Those who came wanting to believe that Zamora really had a UFO encounter were not disappointed. The policeman seemed honest and truthful. One investigator, however, was especially hard to convince. Dr. J. Allen Hynek was an astronomer from Northwestern University in Illinois. He had been a UFO investigator for many years, often working for the air force. Four days after the incident, Dr. Hynek arrived in Socorro. He talked with every witness. He carefully examined the site. Then, after interviewing Lonnie Zamora, Dr. Hynek issued a report. In his opinion, Zamora was "basically sincere, honest, and reliable." In the end, Dr. Hynek called the Socorro encounter one of the "major UFO sightings in the history of the air force's consideration of the subject."

Did Lonnie Zamora see a UFO? Or could the shiny craft have been a secret United States military craft? There was a large military base in the area. But the air force denied that it was testing any secret craft around Socorro. What's more, it had never tested anything that looked like the craft Zamora described. Unable to disprove Zamora's story, the air force reluctantly filed the Socorro sighting as "unidentified."

But there were those who did not believe Lonnie Zamora's story. One doubter was an engineer and writer named Philip J. Klass. Klass believed that most people who reported seeing UFOs were mistaken. What they really saw were known objects, such as weather balloons or planes. Klass visited Socorro two years after the Zamora sighting. After

reviewing the records and talking with witnesses, including Lonnie Zamora, Klass was suspicious. For one thing, he felt that it would have been very difficult for Zamora to see the spaceship and its passengers very clearly from where he was standing. Second, people were living in a house right next to the site. Although the windows of the house were open, they saw and heard nothing.

Klass also thought he found other flaws in Zamora's story. When he talked to Zamora, the policeman's story had changed. He no longer mentioned the blue-orange flame. He remembered only swirling dust. Zamora also talked about a piece of rock that had been partly melted by the flame. If the flame was that hot, Klass reasoned, it should have done a lot more damage to the surrounding grass. Besides, no one but Lonnie Zamora had ever seen the melted rock. He claimed that investigators must have taken it away.

If Philip Klass is right, why did Lonnie Zamora lie about seeing a UFO? What did he have to gain? Klass believed that the

policeman did not lie for himself, but for the good of his town. When word of the UFO landing spread, many people would want to see the site. Tourists would bring much-needed money to Socorro. If that was Lonnie Zamora's intention, his plan worked well, for that is exactly what happened. But many UFO believers feel that the story is reliable. They regard the Socorro sighting as one of the classic UFO cases on record. ■

*If you have been timed while reading this selection, enter your reading time below. Then turn to the Words-per-Minute table on page 154 and look up your reading speed (words per minute). Enter your reading speed on the graph on page 156.*

READING TIME: Unit 6

_____ : _____
*Minutes        Seconds*

# How well did you read?

- *Answer the four types of questions that follow. The directions for each type of question tell you how to mark your answers.*

- *When you have finished all four exercises, check your work by using the answer key on page 150. For each right answer, put a check mark (✓) on the line beside the box. For each wrong answer, write the correct answer on the line.*

- *For scoring each exercise, follow the directions below the questions.*

## A  FINDING THE MAIN IDEA

Look at the three statements below. One expresses the main idea of the story you just read. A good main idea statement answers two questions: it tells *who* or *what* is the subject of the story, and it answers the understood question *does what?* or *is what?* Another statement is *too broad;* it is vague and doesn't tell much about the topic of the story. The third statement is *too narrow;* it tells about only one part of the story.

Match the statements with the three answer choices below by writing the letter of each answer in the box in front of the statement it goes with.

**M—Main Idea**     **B—Too Broad**     **N—Too Narrow**

____ ☐ 1. On April 24, 1964, in Socorro, New Mexico, officer Lonnie Zamora heard a loud roar.

____ ☐ 2. Police officer Lonnie Zamora claimed that he saw a UFO and aliens.

____ ☐ 3. Investigators are divided as to whether or not Zamora actually saw a UFO or if he lied to bring tourism into the town.

____ Score 15 points for a correct *M* answer

____ Score 5 points for each correct *B* or *N* answer

____ TOTAL SCORE:  Finding the Main Idea

## B RECALLING FACTS

How well do you remember the facts in the story you just read?
Put an x in the box in front of the correct answer to each of the
multiple-choice questions below.

1. Lonnie Zamora was a
   - ☐ a. UFO investigator.
   - ☐ b. college professor.
   - ☐ c. police officer.

2. The town of Socorro is located in
   - ☐ a. Illinois.
   - ☐ b. Mexico.
   - ☐ c. New Mexico.

3. One UFO investigator who did not believe the story
   at first was
   - ☐ a. J. Allen Hynek.
   - ☐ b. M. S. Chavez.
   - ☐ c. Lonnie Zamora.

4. The air force termed the Socorro sighting
   - ☐ a. unidentified.
   - ☐ b. untrue.
   - ☐ c. unreported.

5. In general, UFO believers agree with
   - ☐ a. the air force.
   - ☐ b. Lonnie Zamora.
   - ☐ c. Philip Klass.

Score 5 points for each correct answer

_____ TOTAL SCORE: Recalling Facts

## C MAKING INFERENCES

An inference is a judgment that is made or an idea that is arrived
at based on facts or on information that is given. You make an
inference when you understand something that is *not* stated
directly but that is *implied,* or suggested, by the facts that are given.

Below are five statements that are judgments or ideas that have
been arrived at from the facts of the story. Write the letter *C* in
the box in front of each statement that is a correct inference. Write
the letter *F* in front of each faulty inference.

**C—Correct Inference       F—Faulty Inference**

- ☐ 1. Not everyone believes a UFO landed in Socorro.
- ☐ 2. Philip Klass did not like Lonnie Zamora.
- ☐ 3. To his friends, Lonnie Zamora was an honest person.
- ☐ 4. J. Allen Hynek was a thorough investigator.
- ☐ 5. Lonnie Zamora liked to play practical jokes.

Score 5 points for each correct answer

_____ TOTAL SCORE: Making Inferences

## D  USING WORDS PRECISELY

Each of the numbered sentences below contains an underlined word or phrase from the story you have just read. Under the sentence are three definitions. One is a *synonym*, a word that means the same or almost the same thing: *big* and *large*. One is an *antonym*, a word that has the opposite or nearly opposite meaning: *love* and *hate*. One is an unrelated word; it has a completely *different* meaning. Match the definitions with the three answer choices by writing the letter that stands for each answer in the box in front of the definition it goes with.

**S—Synonym    A—Antonym    D—Different**

1. Reluctantly, he stopped the chase to investigate.

   ___ ☐ a. eagerly

   ___ ☐ b. undecidedly

   ___ ☐ c. unwillingly

2. Both men saw large and small indentations in the ground.

   ___ ☐ a. ditches

   ___ ☐ b. dents

   ___ ☐ c. bumps

3. Just before Lonnie Zamora's encounter, the tourist said he had seen a silver craft floating in the air.

   ___ ☐ a. violent clash

   ___ ☐ b. planned meeting

   ___ ☐ c. chance meeting

4. Klass also thought he found other flaws in Zamora's story.

   ___ ☐ a. hidden cracks

   ___ ☐ b. weaknesses

   ___ ☐ c. strengths

5. They regard the Socorro sighting as one of the classic UFO cases on record.

   ___ ☐ a. consider

   ___ ☐ b. enjoy

   ___ ☐ c. disregard

___ Score 3 points for each correct *S* answer

___ Score 1 point for each correct *A* or *D* answer

___ TOTAL SCORE:  Using Words Precisely

● *Enter the four total scores in the spaces below, and add them together to find your Critical Reading Score. Then record your Critical Reading Score on the graph on page 157.*

| | |
|---|---|
| _____ | Finding the Main Idea |
| _____ | Recalling Facts |
| _____ | Making Inferences |
| _____ | Using Words Precisely |
| _____ | **CRITICAL READING SCORE:  Unit 6** |

Norman Muscarello raced into the Exeter, New Hampshire, police station one night to report seeing a UFO with bright red lights. Officer Reginald Toland, seated, listened to Muscarello's story, probably not believing a word of it. But when officers David Hunt, at left, and Eugene Bertrand, far right, saw the UFO too, Toland knew something weird was definitely going on.

# Incident at Exeter

Eighteen-year-old Norman Muscarello was tired. After leaving a friend's home in Amesbury, Massachusetts, on September 3, 1965, he had hoped to hitch a ride back to his home in Exeter, New Hampshire, about 12 miles away. But traffic had been light on Route 150 and Norman was out of luck. Now, at 2:00 A.M., he still had a few miles to go before he could crawl into bed. Little did he realize how many hours away that would be!

As he passed an open field, Muscarello suddenly stopped dead in his tracks. He watched in disbelief as a huge round object emerged from behind some trees and rose above the field. It had pulsing red lights that glowed so brightly that Muscarello could not see any structure behind them. The young man guessed that the thing was about 80 or 90 feet long. It made no sound at all and seemed almost clumsy in its movements.

At first the object hovered over a house that belonged to Clyde Russell, bathing it in brilliant red light. Then it seemed to wobble toward Muscarello, coming so close that he dived into a ditch along the side of the road. Finally, the object backed off a bit. Terrified, Muscarello scrambled from the ditch and ran to the Russell house. Banging on the door, he shouted for help. When no one answered, Muscarello ran back to the road, hoping to flag down an approaching car. This time he was in luck. The car stopped, and the driver agreed to take the frightened young man to the Exeter police station.

"It was as big as a house!" Muscarello told Reginald Toland, the police officer on duty that night. Although officer Toland was skeptical, he agreed to call in a police car to investigate.

The officer who answered the call, Eugene Bertrand, had his own story to tell. An hour earlier, he had noticed a car parked on the side of the highway about two miles outside of Exeter. He stopped to investigate. The driver, a woman, was badly frightened. She told the officer that her car had been followed for miles by a silent object with flashing red lights.

"That sounds exactly like what I saw!" said Muscarello.

Were both witnesses imagining things? Officer Bertrand was pretty sure that what they had seen was a helicopter or some other conventional aircraft. But he agreed to follow Muscarello back to the field where he had sighted the object.

At first everything at the field appeared normal. As they walked along, stars twinkled in the clear night sky. Suddenly Muscarello shouted, "I see it! I see it!" Officer Bertrand watched in amazement as a huge round object rose above some trees. It hovered silently, its brilliant red lights lighting up the field.

"It was about 100 feet in the air, and about 200 feet away from us," the officer recalled. "I could see five bright red lights in a straight row. They dimmed from right to left, and then from left to right—just like an advertising sign does."

Racing back to the police car, Bertrand radioed for immediate assistance. The two men were soon joined by officer David Hunt, who arrived just in time to see the object leave. "It sort of floated and wobbled," said officer Hunt. Then "it started moving, slow-like, across the tops of the trees, just above the trees. It was rocking when it did this. A creepy type of look. Airplanes don't do this."

The men watched as the object moved toward the ocean. After it disappeared a B-47 aircraft flew over. "You could tell the difference," said Hunt. "There was no comparison." Officer Bertrand later described his reaction. "Your mind is telling you this can't be true, and yet you're seeing it . . . I have never seen an aircraft like that before, and I know . . . they haven't changed that much since I was in the service."

Officer Hunt agreed. "My brain kept telling me that this doesn't happen—but it was, right in front of my eyes. . . . I don't know what it was. All I can say is that it was there, and three of us saw it together."

Back at the Exeter police station, officer

Toland was having a busy night. No sooner had he received the report from Bertrand than he got a call from a night telephone operator. A man calling from a telephone booth in the nearby town of Hampton had claimed that a flying saucer was heading directly toward him. For some reason the connection was broken, and the call could not be traced.

Although the incident received some local publicity, interest seemed to fade rather quickly. Officials from Pease Air Force Base, about 10 miles away, interviewed Muscarello, Bertrand, and Hunt, but the air force declined to make an official comment. The story might have died completely if a reporter named John Fuller had not taken an interest. A writer for the magazine *Saturday Review,* Fuller went to Exeter and started asking questions. What he learned changed him from "a friendly skeptic" to a UFO believer.

After talking with Muscarello, Bertrand, and Hunt, Fuller was impressed with their honesty. He also interviewed many other people who had either seen the same UFO or something very much like it. Fuller's

conclusion: the UFO reports came from too many reliable sources to doubt.

One of those sources was Virginia Hale, a local newspaper reporter. She told Fuller that she had glanced out her kitchen window and had seen a large bright object stop and hover over a neighbor's house. It was dome-shaped but flat on the bottom and had a bluish green glow, reminding her of neon lights.

Joseph Jalbert had seen a reddish cigar-shaped object high over the power lines near his house. After it hovered for several minutes, it released a reddish orange disk that zigzagged down over the power lines. Jalbert watched a silver pipe extend from the disk to touch the power lines for a minute or so, then draw back into the disk. The disk returned to the larger object and seemed to disappear inside it.

Jalbert's sighting was typical of many that Fuller investigated. In all, 73 reports involved power lines. Was this just a coincidence?

* * *

Many people have dismissed the air force versions of what happened. Officials first

claimed that the witnesses saw "stars and planets twinkling." When most people rejected that explanation, the air force claimed that it must have been a military exercise. Yet all flight missions at the base were over before 2:00 that morning. The air force can't explain what all those witnesses saw that early morning in September. What happened at Exeter is still a mystery. ∎

*If you have been timed while reading this selection, enter your reading time below. Then turn to the Words-per-Minute table on page 154 and look up your reading speed (words per minute). Enter your reading speed on the graph on page 156.*

READING TIME: Unit 7

_____ : _____
*Minutes*     *Seconds*

# How well did you read?

- *Answer the four types of questions that follow. The directions for each type of question tell you how to mark your answers.*

- *When you have finished all four exercises, check your work by using the answer key on page 150. For each right answer, put a check mark (✓) on the line beside the box. For each wrong answer, write the correct answer on the line.*

- *For scoring each exercise, follow the directions below the questions.*

## A  FINDING THE MAIN IDEA

Look at the three statements below. One expresses the main idea of the story you just read. A good main idea statement answers two questions: it tells *who* or *what* is the subject of the story, and it answers the understood question *does what?* or *is what?* Another statement is *too broad;* it is vague and doesn't tell much about the topic of the story. The third statement is *too narrow;* it tells about only one part of the story.

   Match the statements with the three answer choices below by writing the letter of each answer in the box in front of the statement it goes with.

**M—Main Idea      B—Too Broad      N—Too Narrow**

____ ☐ 1. The air force can't explain the UFO that Norman Muscarello and several others say they saw in Exeter, New Hampshire, in September 1965.

____ ☐ 2. A UFO sighting in Exeter, New Hampshire, drew the attention of many people in 1965.

____ ☐ 3. Norman Muscarello left his friend's home in Amesbury and tried to hitch a ride home to Exeter, New Hampshire.

____ Score 15 points for a correct *M* answer
____ Score 5 points for each correct *B* or *N* answer
____ **TOTAL SCORE:** Finding the Main Idea

## B  RECALLING FACTS

How well do you remember the facts in the story you just read? Put an x in the box in front of the correct answer to each of the multiple-choice questions below.

1. Muscarello first reported his UFO sighting to
   - ☐ a. the air force.
   - ☐ b. the Exeter police.
   - ☐ c. John Fuller.

2. Police officer Eugene Bertrand
   - ☐ a. laughed at Muscarello's reported sighting.
   - ☐ b. saw the same thing Muscarello did.
   - ☐ c. was afraid to investigate the supposed sighting.

3. One police officer who saw the UFO was
   - ☐ a. Virginia Hale.
   - ☐ b. David Hunt.
   - ☐ c. John Fuller.

4. The air force
   - ☐ a. denied there were UFOs in the area.
   - ☐ b. agreed with Muscarello.
   - ☐ c. declined to make any official comment.

5. John Fuller's investigation revealed that
   - ☐ a. UFOs couldn't possibly exist.
   - ☐ b. Muscarello was not telling the truth.
   - ☐ c. many reliable, believable people claimed to have seen a UFO.

Score 5 points for each correct answer

_____ TOTAL SCORE: Recalling Facts

## C  MAKING INFERENCES

An inference is a judgment that is made or an idea that is arrived at based on facts or on information that is given. You make an inference when you understand something that is *not* stated directly but that is *implied*, or suggested, by the facts that are given.

Below are five statements that are judgments or ideas that have been arrived at from the facts of the story. Write the letter C in the box in front of each statement that is a correct inference. Write the letter F in front of each faulty inference.

**C—Correct Inference      F—Faulty Inference**

1. At first Eugene Bertrand did not believe there was an actual UFO sighting.

2. John Fuller was impressed by Norman Muscarello's honesty.

3. People in New Hampshire have lively imaginations.

4. John Fuller was a curious person.

5. Most people accept the air force versions of what happened in Exeter.

Score 5 points for each correct answer

_____ TOTAL SCORE: Making Inferences

## D USING WORDS PRECISELY

Each of the numbered sentences below contains an underlined word or phrase from the story you have just read. Under the sentence are three definitions. One is a *synonym*, a word that means the same or almost the same thing: *big* and *large*. One is an *antonym*, a word that has the opposite or nearly opposite meaning: *love* and *hate*. One is an unrelated word; it has a completely *different* meaning. Match the definitions with the three answer choices by writing the letter that stands for each answer in the box in front of the definition it goes with.

**S—Synonym     A—Antonym     D—Different**

1. It had <u>pulsing</u> red lights that glowed so brightly that Muscarello could not see any structure behind them.

____ ☐ a. constant; fixed

____ ☐ b. regular beat or flash

____ ☐ c. heart beats

2. Officer Bertrand was pretty sure that what they had seen was a helicopter or some other <u>conventional</u> aircraft.

____ ☐ a. usual kind

____ ☐ b. different; unique

____ ☐ c. following custom or tradition

3. Jalbert's sighting was <u>typical</u> of many that Fuller investigated.

____ ☐ a. ordinary

____ ☐ b. of a type; regular

____ ☐ c. rare; unusual

4. In all, 73 reports involved power lines. Was this just a <u>coincidence</u>?

____ ☐ a. happens at same time

____ ☐ b. agreement

____ ☐ c. unrelated events

5. Many people have <u>dismissed</u> the air force versions of what happened.

____ ☐ a. thought about seriously

____ ☐ b. allowed to go

____ ☐ c. put out of mind

____ Score 3 points for each correct *S* answer
____ Score 1 point for each correct *A* or *D* answer
____ TOTAL SCORE: Using Words Precisely

● *Enter the four total scores in the spaces below, and add them together to find your Critical Reading Score. Then record your Critical Reading Score on the graph on page 157.*

| | |
|---|---|
| _____ | Finding the Main Idea |
| _____ | Recalling Facts |
| _____ | Making Inferences |
| _____ | Using Words Precisely |
| _____ | CRITICAL READING SCORE: Unit 7 |

# GROUP TWO

A little girl named Kimberly Baker startled everyone with her story about the "bubble." She insisted that a shiny object floated toward her in a grassy field one afternoon before landing just a few yards away. Mrs. Baker and Allie King, a family friend, believed the sighting was not a child's fantasy. But was the "bubble" a UFO? Only Kimberly knows for sure.

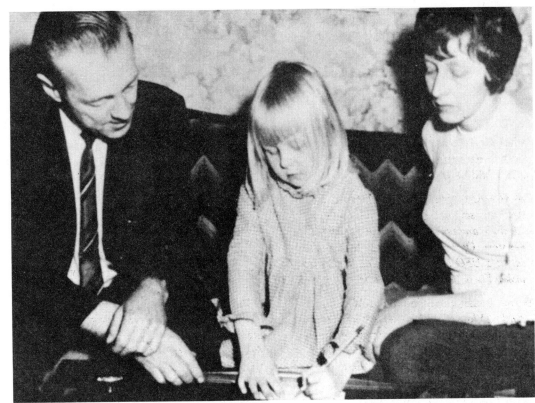

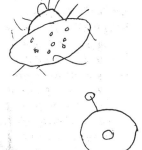

# Kim's Story

Richard Bonenfant, a UFO investigator, headed for the town of Bingham, Maine, when he heard the news. He had a hunch that it would be worth checking out.

*BINGHAM—She's just six years old but states she saw a UFO on the afternoon of April 23, and nobody has been able to 'shake' her story. Of course, Kimberly Baker doesn't call it a UFO or a flying saucer. To her it looked like a 'big ball' or a 'bubble.' . . .*

The news story appeared in the *Morning Sentinel* of Waterville, Maine. It said that the field in which Kimberly reported the sighting "appeared as if some object might have landed on it, for grass and close-to-ground greenery was flattened."

Bonenfant wondered if Kimberly could be a reliable witness. Or was her story merely a figment of her imagination? The following account is based on his report.

* * *

According to Kim, on April 23, 1966, she and her two cousins, Wendy and Bruce, had walked to a field near her cousins' house to pick pussy willows. When they found the stems were too strong to break off by hand, Wendy and Bruce headed back to their house for a pair of scissors. That was the moment Kimberly first noticed a large, shiny object floating toward her. Too frightened to move, she watched as the object landed a few yards away. For more than a minute Kimberly stared at the thing, expecting something—anything—to happen. Instead, it suddenly rose into the air and flew off over the roof of a neighbor's house as silently as it had come.

When the little girl returned home, she tried to tell her mother what she had seen.

"Mommy, Mommy, I saw something!" Kimberly cried excitedly, tugging at her mother's skirt.

But Mrs. Baker had other things on her mind that day and did not pay much attention to her daughter's pleadings. Two days later, though, Mrs. Baker remembered Kimberly's excitement and stopped to ask her about it.

"What did you see?" asked Mrs. Baker.

"A big bubble."

Kimberly went on to describe the size and color of the "bubble." It was "like Daddy's car but higher," she said, adding that it was "shiny, like the toaster in the kitchen." In answering her mother's questions, Kimberly revealed that the object also had a door and a rectangular-shaped window about eight inches high. Each end of the object was set off by red lights. A flashing green light was fixed just above the center of the object. Asked if she could draw a picture of the object, Kimberly readily complied.

Mrs. Baker did not think her daughter's experience was some fantasy she had thought up. Yet she was uncertain what to do. Finally she called on a family friend, Allie King. King worked for the Gannett Publishing Company, which owned a number of newspapers.

On April 27 Allie King talked with Kimberly about the experience. Although King tried time and again to confuse the young girl, she never once wavered from her story. During King's questioning, however, something quite unexpected came up.

"Were you afraid when you saw the bubble?" Kimberly was asked.

"At first I was," she answered, "but not after the man smiled at me."

Allie King and Mrs. Baker were startled by that statement. This was the first time Kimberly mentioned a man in connection with the sighting. Mrs. Baker tried to hide the nervousness in her voice.

"What did the man look like, Kimberly?" she asked.

Kimberly said the man resembled her father, or a family friend named René. Dressed in "shiny white," the man had "lots of black buttons on his chest." After removing what appeared to be a "bubble" on his head, the man winked and smiled. Then Kimberly said she saw his lips move as if he were trying to say something, although no sounds came forth.

Kimberly then led her mother and Allie King to the field where the craft had landed. Even days later, a circular area of flattened grass about 15 feet in diameter was still clearly visible. Within the circle pussy willow stems had been broken off. Instead of their usual whitish-yellow color, these stems were dark, as if they had been burned.

Impressed by Kimberly's story, and by the evidence in the field, Allie King called in a reporter from the *Morning Sentinel*. On May 4 reporter Richard Plummer talked with Kimberly. Once again, her story was the same in every detail. Yet Mrs. Baker was in store for another surprise when she asked her daughter if anyone else had seen the "bubble."

"Yes," Kim answered. "A dog saw it, and he barked, too!"

Later a neighbor confirmed that a mongrel had created quite a din the Saturday afternoon of Kimberly's sighting, but the neighbor had ignored the dog's constant barking.

\* \* \*

Did Kimberly Baker have a UFO encounter? Bonenfant talked at length with her and visited the landing site himself. He is convinced that Kimberly was a reliable witness, and that what she saw was not a conventional aircraft. His evaluation of the sighting: UNKNOWN, meaning he felt what Kimberly saw was not of this Earth. ■

*If you have been timed while reading this selection, enter your reading time below. Then turn to the Words-per-Minute table on page 155 and look up your reading speed (words per minute). Enter your reading speed on the graph on page 156.*

READING TIME: Unit 8

_____ : _____
*Minutes*       *Seconds*

# How well did you read?

- *Answer the four types of questions that follow. The directions for each type of question tell you how to mark your answers.*

- *When you have finished all four exercises, check your work by using the answer key on page 151. For each right answer, put a check mark (✓) on the line beside the box. For each wrong answer, write the correct answer on the line.*

- *For scoring each exercise, follow the directions below the questions.*

## A  FINDING THE MAIN IDEA

Look at the three statements below. One expresses the main idea of the story you just read. A good main idea statement answers two questions: it tells *who* or *what* is the subject of the story, and it answers the understood question *does what?* or *is what?* Another statement is *too broad;* it is vague and doesn't tell much about the topic of the story. The third statement is *too narrow;* it tells about only one part of the story.

Match the statements with the three answer choices below by writing the letter of each answer in the box in front of the statement it goes with.

**M—Main Idea**      **B—Too Broad**      **N—Too Narrow**

____  ☐  1. A UFO sighting was reported in Maine in 1966.

____  ☐  2. A UFO investigator and a reporter believe that Kimberly Baker experienced a UFO encounter.

____  ☐  3. Kimberly Baker told her mother she saw a "bubble" land in a field near her cousins' house.

____  Score 15 points for a correct *M* answer

____  Score 5 points for each correct *B* or *N* answer

____  TOTAL SCORE:  Finding the Main Idea

## B RECALLING FACTS

How well do you remember the facts in the story you just read? Put an *x* in the box in front of the correct answer to each of the multiple-choice questions below.

1. The *Morning Sentinel* was the name of a
   - ____ ☐ a. book written about Kimberly Baker.
   - ____ ☐ b. newspaper in Waterville, Maine.
   - ____ ☐ c. story written about a UFO encounter.

2. When Kimberly first saw the object floating toward her, she
   - ____ ☐ a. cried out in excitement.
   - ____ ☐ b. was afraid.
   - ____ ☐ c. ran home to her mother.

3. Mrs. Baker thought her daughter's story was
   - ____ ☐ a. made up.
   - ____ ☐ b. not a fantasy.
   - ____ ☐ c. told to Kimberly by her cousins.

4. Allie King was
   - ____ ☐ a. a friend of the Bakers.
   - ____ ☐ b. a newspaper reporter.
   - ____ ☐ c. owner of the Gannett Publishing Company.

5. In the end Kimberly's story
   - ____ ☐ a. turned out to be false.
   - ____ ☐ b. had changed many times in the telling.
   - ____ ☐ c. was believed by several people.

Score 5 points for each correct answer

____ TOTAL SCORE: Recalling Facts

## C MAKING INFERENCES

An inference is a judgment that is made or an idea that is arrived at based on facts or on information that is given. You make an inference when you understand something that is *not* stated directly but that is *implied*, or suggested, by the facts that are given.

Below are five statements that are judgments or ideas that have been arrived at from the facts of the story. Write the letter *C* in the box in front of each statement that is a correct inference. Write the letter *F* in front of each faulty inference.

**C—Correct Inference     F—Faulty Inference**

- ____ ☐ 1. Kimberly Baker liked to make up stories about things she saw.
- ____ ☐ 2. Kimberly and her cousins were friends.
- ____ ☐ 3. Mrs. Baker rarely paid attention to her daughter.
- ____ ☐ 4. Kimberly was an observant child.
- ____ ☐ 5. Richard Bonenfant was impressed with Kimberly.

Score 5 points for each correct answer

____ TOTAL SCORE: Making Inferences

## D USING WORDS PRECISELY

Each of the numbered sentences below contains an underlined word or phrase from the story you have just read. Under the sentence are three definitions. One is a *synonym*, a word that means the same or almost the same thing: *big* and *large*. One is an *antonym*, a word that has the opposite or nearly opposite meaning: *love* and *hate*. One is an unrelated word; it has a completely *different* meaning. Match the definitions with the three answer choices by writing the letter that stands for each answer in the box in front of the definition it goes with.

**S—Synonym     A—Antonym     D—Different**

1. Or was her [Kimberly's] story merely a <u>figment of her imagination</u>?

____ ☐ a. something imagined

____ ☐ b. a fact

____ ☐ c. a fable

2. Asked if she could draw a picture of the object, Kimberly readily <u>complied</u>.

____ ☐ a. refused

____ ☐ b. agreed with

____ ☐ c. commanded

3. Although King tried time and again to confuse the young girl, she never once <u>wavered</u> from her story.

____ ☐ a. flickered

____ ☐ b. stood fast

____ ☐ c. hesitated

4. Yet Mrs. Baker was <u>in store</u> for another surprise when she asked her daughter if anyone else had seen the "bubble."

____ ☐ a. at once; presently

____ ☐ b. on hand

____ ☐ c. waiting in the future

5. . . . a neighbor confirmed that a mongrel had created quite a <u>din</u> . . . but [she] had ignored the dog's constant barking.

____ ☐ a. loud noises

____ ☐ b. sounds

____ ☐ c. silence

____ Score 3 points for each correct *S* answer

____ Score 1 point for each correct *A* or *D* answer

____ TOTAL SCORE: Using Words Precisely

● *Enter the four total scores in the spaces below, and add them together to find your Critical Reading Score. Then record your Critical Reading Score on the graph on page 157.*

_____ Finding the Main Idea
_____ Recalling Facts
_____ Making Inferences
_____ Using Words Precisely

_____ CRITICAL READING SCORE:  Unit 8

*Betty Andreasson has no proof that she was abducted by aliens in January 1967. Only under hypnosis did she remember the oval spacecraft she boarded in her backyard, the 15-foot bird that looked like an eagle, and Quazgaa, the alien leader (shown on next page). Betty drew a picture of the eagle from memory and helped an artist design a likeness of Quazgaa.*

**Betty stood about this tall before the bird.**

# The Secrets of Betty Andreasson

Betty Andreasson knew that something incredible had happened on that winter night in 1967. But what? For many years, she could remember almost nothing. Then it all came tumbling out. She had been kidnapped by creatures from outer space!

The evening of January 25, 1967, started out quietly enough. A fog had settled in, wrapping the small town of South Ashburnham, Massachusetts, in an eerie cocoon. Betty, her parents, and her seven children were at home. Betty's husband, who had been badly hurt in a car accident the month before, was still in the hospital.

Suddenly, the lights in the house began to flicker. Then all was dark. At the same time Betty noticed a strange pink glow pulsing through the kitchen window. Her father saw something even stranger outside: "creatures . . . just like Halloween freaks. I thought they had put on a funny kind of headdress imitating a moon man . . . the one in front looked at me and I felt kind of queer." After that, he remembered nothing. But Betty watched, horrified, as the creatures moved into the house. They didn't use the door, however. Instead, they passed right through the walls!

For more than 10 years that was all Betty could recall about the incident. But the

memory nagged at her. She began reading about other people who had had experiences much like hers. Those people could remember the details only under hypnosis. Would hypnosis also help her? Finally, in 1977, Betty agreed to a series of sessions with a hypnotist. The story that emerged during those sessions is one of the most bizarre in UFO history.

What happened after the creatures entered the Andreasson kitchen? Only Betty witnessed the following events. Her parents and children were put into some kind of trance. Betty watched in amazement as short, gray-skinned aliens lined up before her. Dressed in shiny, form-fitting uniforms, they had large, slanted eyes. Each hand had only three fingers.

Although the aliens never spoke, Betty was able to understand their thoughts. "We need food for our minds," their leader, whose name was Quazgaa, told her. A deeply religious woman, Betty gave the creature a Bible.

"Follow us," they ordered, "so that you can help the world." Unable to resist, Betty followed the creatures to her backyard, where an oval spacecraft hovered a few inches off the ground.

Betty was led to a brightly lit room on board the craft. Then she was forced to endure a very unpleasant medical exam.

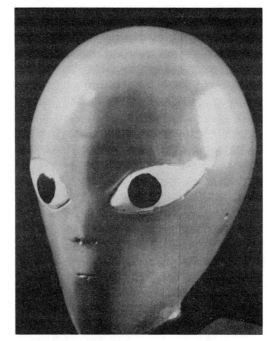

A number of thin wires were inserted into her body. According to Betty, the aliens relieved the pain the wires caused by placing their hands on her forehead. After the exam, she was led through a long black tunnel into a second room. There she was placed inside a glass canopy. Then her body was smeared with a gray fluid that protected her while the craft traveled through space.

When they reached the end of their

journey, Betty was led through a series of tunnels, finally stepping out into an eerie, lifeless landscape. Two aliens guided her along a floating track between square buildings. Betty recalled being surrounded by shimmering red lights. Horrifying creatures without heads swarmed around the three travelers.

Then the scenery improved somewhat. Following along a path, Betty noticed misty bodies of water on either side of her, and ahead, at the end of the path, a pyramid. In front of her floating crystals reflected a brilliant light, which was obscured by an incredible vision.

"I'm standing before a large bird," Betty later reported. "It's very warm. . . . And that bird looks like an eagle to me. And it's living! It has a white head and there is light in back of it—real, white light. . . . The light seems so bright in back of it. It's a beautiful, bright light. . . . The light just keeps getting bigger and bigger. Oh, the heat is so strong!"

As Betty watched, the huge bird vanished, leaving in its place a small fire. When the fire died, a fat gray worm crawled out from the ashes.

What did these visions represent? Betty Andreasson was mystified.

"Do you understand?" she was asked.

"No, I don't understand what this is all about, or why I'm even here," she answered.

"You have been chosen," a voice told her.

But what she had been chosen for was not explained.

Eventually Betty was brought back to the room with the glass canopy. There Quazgaa told her that he would give her certain information that could help humans. He said further that the secrets she had learned "had been locked in your mind."

It seemed to Betty that hours had passed. But it was still nighttime when she was returned to her backyard. Inside the house her family was still frozen in a trance. Before departing, the aliens led them all to their beds.

When she awoke in the morning, Betty could remember little about the night before. And that is where the matter rested until hypnosis unlocked the secrets in her mind. Did the events of January 25 take place as Betty Andreasson described them? Many people who have heard her story believe that she is insane. However, doctors who have examined her conclude that Betty is sane. Another investigator described her as "honest" and "sincere."

Betty Andreasson is not alone in claiming that she has been abducted by aliens. Both before and after her story was made public, hundreds of others made similar claims that they were also taken by aliens. Like Betty, most people who report their abductions recall being led into a brightly lit room and subjected to a painful physical exam. Yet Betty's story is unique because no one else has ever described the images that she reported seeing on the strange planet. But, other than the fleeting impressions that her family can recall, Betty has no proof that she is telling the truth. Nor can she remember the vital information Quazgaa gave her. Perhaps that is one secret that will remain forever locked in her mind. ■

*If you have been timed while reading this selection, enter your reading time below. Then turn to the Words-per-Minute table on page 155 and look up your reading speed (words per minute). Enter your reading speed on the graph on page 156.*

READING TIME: Unit 9

_____ : _____
*Minutes          Seconds*

# How well did you read?

- *Answer the four types of questions that follow. The directions for each type of question tell you how to mark your answers.*

- *When you have finished all four exercises, check your work by using the answer key on page 151. For each right answer, put a check mark (✓) on the line beside the box. For each wrong answer, write the correct answer on the line.*

- *For scoring each exercise, follow the directions below the questions.*

## A  FINDING THE MAIN IDEA

Look at the three statements below. One expresses the main idea of the story you just read. A good main idea statement answers two questions: it tells *who* or *what* is the subject of the story, and it answers the understood question *does what?* or *is what?* Another statement is *too broad;* it is vague and doesn't tell much about the topic of the story. The third statement is *too narrow;* it tells about only one part of the story.

Match the statements with the three answer choices below by writing the letter of each answer in the box in front of the statement it goes with.

**M—Main Idea     B—Too Broad     N—Too Narrow**

_____ ☐ 1. Some people who have claimed to have UFO encounters have also been abducted by aliens.

_____ ☐ 2. Betty Andreasson claims that only hypnosis helped her to remember her 1967 UFO encounter.

_____ ☐ 3. Betty Andreasson claims to have been abducted by aliens, but she hasn't been able to prove her story.

_____ Score 15 points for a correct *M* answer
_____ Score 5 points for each correct *B* or *N* answer
___ TOTAL SCORE: Finding the Main Idea

## B  RECALLING FACTS

How well do you remember the facts in the story you just read?
Put an *x* in the box in front of the correct answer to each of the
multiple-choice questions below.

1. Betty Andreasson's UFO encounter took place in
   - ___ ☐ a. January 1967.
   - ___ ☐ b. June 1977.
   - ___ ☐ c. September 1987.

2. When Betty was abducted, she was
   - ___ ☐ a. alone in her parents' house.
   - ___ ☐ b. visiting her husband in the hospital.
   - ___ ☐ c. at home with her children and her parents.

3. Betty recalled the details of her abduction only after
   - ___ ☐ a. a long stay in a hospital.
   - ___ ☐ b. undergoing hypnosis.
   - ___ ☐ c. her parents talked to her about the incident.

4. The bird Betty claims she saw during her abduction was
   - ___ ☐ a. an eagle.
   - ___ ☐ b. an owl.
   - ___ ☐ c. a UFO.

5. To Betty the abduction seemed to last
   - ___ ☐ a. only minutes.
   - ___ ☐ b. several hours.
   - ___ ☐ c. a lifetime.

Score 5 points for each correct answer

___ TOTAL SCORE:  Recalling Facts

## C  MAKING INFERENCES

An inference is a judgment that is made or an idea that is arrived
at based on facts or on information that is given. You make an
inference when you understand something that is *not* stated
directly but that is *implied*, or suggested, by the facts that are given.

Below are five statements that are judgments or ideas that have
been arrived at from the facts of the story. Write the letter *C* in
the box in front of each statement that is a correct inference. Write
the letter *F* in front of each faulty inference.

**C—Correct Inference     F—Faulty Inference**

- ___ ☐ 1. The aliens were more interested in Betty than in her parents or her children.
- ___ ☐ 2. Betty was happy that the aliens chose her.
- ___ ☐ 3. Betty did not have a very good memory.
- ___ ☐ 4. Betty didn't want anyone to know what had happened to her.
- ___ ☐ 5. Betty can't remember everything the alien told her.

Score 5 points for each correct answer

___ TOTAL SCORE:  Making Inferences

## D   USING WORDS PRECISELY

Each of the numbered sentences below contains an underlined word or phrase from the story you have just read. Under the sentence are three definitions. One is a *synonym,* a word that means the same or almost the same thing: *big* and *large.* One is an *antonym,* a word that has the opposite or nearly opposite meaning: *love* and *hate.* One is an unrelated word; it has a completely *different* meaning. Match the definitions with the three answer choices by writing the letter that stands for each answer in the box in front of the definition it goes with.

**S—Synonym      A—Antonym      D—Different**

1. The story that emerged . . . is one of the most <u>bizarre</u> in UFO history.

____ ☐ a. odd

____ ☐ b. common

____ ☐ c. great

2. Then she was forced to <u>endure</u> a very unpleasant medical exam.

____ ☐ a. surrender

____ ☐ b. support

____ ☐ c. put up with

3. In front of her floating crystals reflected a brilliant light, which was <u>obscured</u> by an incredible vision.

____ ☐ a. hidden

____ ☐ b. misunderstood

____ ☐ c. clear

4. Betty Andreasson is not alone in claiming that she has been <u>abducted</u> by aliens.

____ ☐ a. moved apart

____ ☐ b. freed

____ ☐ c. kidnapped

5. Yet Betty's story is <u>unique</u> because no one else has ever described the images that she reported seeing on the strange planet.

____ ☐ a. different

____ ☐ b. one of a kind

____ ☐ c. ordinary

____ Score 3 points for each correct *S* answer

____ Score 1 point for each correct *A* or *D* answer

____ TOTAL SCORE: Using Words Precisely

● *Enter the four total scores in the spaces below, and add them together to find your Critical Reading Score. Then record your Critical Reading Score on the graph on page 157.*

_____ Finding the Main Idea
_____ Recalling Facts
_____ Making Inferences
_____ Using Words Precisely

_____ CRITICAL READING SCORE:  Unit 9

# 'Glowing UFO' Sighted by Ashland Policeman

### By DICK MEZZY

Ashland — The first time something like this happened around here was 70 years ago.

A man described a "football-shaped" object hovering in the sky with red blinking lights. Either history is repeating itself as it sometimes has a habit of doing or what Ashland Policeman Herbert L. Schirmer saw was an unidentified flying object.

Schi___ __, a Navy vet___ __ __er of the po____ ___ __ __for seven ___ ___ is patrol ____ ___ight just

___ __O inter-
___ __be-

___ Wla-
___nday
___ __the

___ _ght to
__what he
___ubt him
___ hing and
__ y he saw

___ and Schirm-
___ he area and
___ . . . on the
___ d what they
___ ___ a bit
___ ___ ne

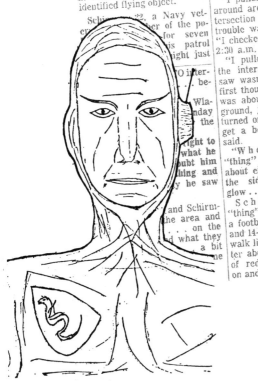

the way he would start any other Saturday night patrol.

Driving south from Ashland on Hwy. 6 he neared the junction of Hwy. 6-63. The time was almost 2:30 a.m. Sunday.

As he neared the intersection he saw the glow of red lights coming from the Hwy. 63 side of the intersection, just north of the junction.

### 'It Was 2:30'

"I pulled into a little turn-around area just past the intersection to see what the trouble was," Schirmer said, "I checked my watch; it was 2:30 a.m.

"I pulled over the rise of the intersection and what I saw wasn't a truck as I had first thought . . . the "thing" was about 6-8 feet off the ground, just hanging there. I turned on my bright lights to get a better look at it," he said.

"When I did that, the "thing" started to glow and about eight red lights around the side of it started to glow . . ."

Schirmer described the "thing" as being shaped like a football, about 20 feet long, and 14-15 feet high, with a catwalk like ring around the center above which was a series of red lights which blinked on and off.

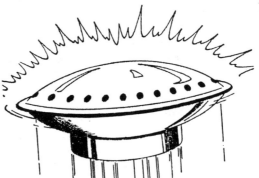

Sketch of UFO as Herbert Shirmer described it.

We plan to have it tested to find out what it is, the chief said. "I hope it answers the question if it is part of the 'thing.'"

### Test Requested

A lie-detector test has been requested by the young patrolman. The test will be conducted in Omaha as soon as arrangements can be made for it.

"The results of the tests," Chief Wlaschin said, "will be made public as soon as they are completed . . . win, draw or loose . . ."

wasn't the way he saw it and I have faith in him that he saw something. If he says it was a flying saucer . . . well, it must have been a flying saucer. I'm going to back him all the way and stick my neck out for him," Wlaschin said.

The chief said they notified the U.S. Air Force at Offutt AFB Monday of the incident but as yet had not received any response.

### 1897 Sightings

In April, 1897, a group of people returning from church one Sunday evening saw an object in the sky with a bright, pulsating light, traveling northward from Ashland at a high rate of speed.

(From February to April of that year, several reports of sightings came from towns from Hastings to Omaha. All of them described the same type of object).

According to the young policeman he watched the object for a few seconds as it rose to a height of about 50 feet. The next thing he heard was a sound like a "pulsating siren" only weirder. "Then it shot straight up and disappeared."

### 'Believe It or Not'

Schirmer said when he returned to the station, about a mile away, he noticed it was 3 a.m. At the end of his shift

*While patrolling the highway early one morning in Ashland, Nebraska, officer Herbert Schirmer spotted a row of flickering lights. He pulled over for a closer look . . . Half an hour later, Schirmer recorded in his logbook: "Saw a flying saucer at the junction of highways 6 and 63. Believe it or not." But there was more, much more, to Schirmer's UFO encounter. He drew these sketches as proof of his experience.*

# Encounter in Nebraska

"Believe it or not." With those words, patrolman Herbert Schirmer summed up his police report describing what had happened just half an hour earlier. At 2:30 A.M. on December 3, 1967, officer Schirmer saw the UFO.

The facts in the police report did not make much of a story. The 22-year-old police officer was driving on Highway 63 in Ashland, Nebraska, when he saw a row of flickering lights ahead. It must be a truck, he thought, turning on the high beams in his cruiser. As if in response, the object shot off into the sky and disappeared. What officer Schirmer did not include in his report, and what he himself did not find out until much later, was the rest of the story.

As scanty as the report's details were, they excited the interest of UFO investigators. After talking with the young patrolman, their interest grew even stronger. Officer Schirmer revealed that following the incident he had been bothered by a headache. A buzzing noise in his head had kept him from sleeping. What's more, he had a red welt under his left ear that he could not explain. Nor could he account for a 29-minute period of time. Almost half an hour had disappeared from his memory.

The UFO investigators have heard similar stories before. Many people who claim to have encounters with UFOs often experience odd physical symptoms. They also all seem to suffer from lapses of time that they cannot account for. If officer Schirmer would agree to be hypnotized, perhaps he, like other victims, would remember what had happened.

Somewhat doubtful, Schirmer nonetheless agreed to try hypnosis. He never dreamed how startling the results would be.

Once he was in a trance, the young officer remembered the event clearly. He watched the UFO take off. Then he decided to follow it. Driving up a dirt road, he suddenly slammed on the brakes. There it was—a metallic, football-shaped craft lit by a silvery glow! As it hovered over a field, its lights flickered rapidly, and it made a "whooshing" sound. At that point officer Schirmer tried to call in a report to the police at Wahoo. But his radio would not work. His lights and car engine also quit.

Schirmer continued to stare as the landing gear extended, and the object finally landed in the field. Several beings stepped from the craft and headed toward him. They were shooting some kind of green-colored gas at him! The officer wanted to draw his gun but was prevented by some kind of mental block. Then one of the beings turned a bright ray on Schirmer, causing him to pass out.

The next thing Schirmer remembered was being forced to roll down his car window. One of the creatures, who looked quite human at close range, pressed something against his neck.

"Are you the watchman over this place?" asked the alien, pointing to a power plant. "Is this the only source of power you have?"

Later the beings revealed they needed electric power to run their craft. When officer Schirmer had interrupted them, they had been stealing electricity from overhead power lines.

"Would you shoot at a spaceship?" the being asked. When Schirmer said that he would not, he was invited on board the UFO.

Inside the craft Schirmer saw creatures dressed in close-fitting silver uniforms with hoods fitted with antennae. An emblem on the uniforms resembled a winged serpent. Although the beings were only about five feet tall, they were muscular, with chests larger than those of most humans. Their heads were strangely thin and elongated. Slightly slanted eyes, which Schirmer described as "like a cat's eyes," dominated their faces. Flat noses, mouths like slits, and grayish-white complexions added to their eerie appearance.

The spacecraft itself contained control panels and machines that looked like computers to Schirmer. One of the aliens pushed a button and pictures were projected on a screen. Schirmer began to grow uncomfortable. "Through my mind . . . somehow . . . he is telling me things. . . . My mind hurts. . . ."

The aliens seemed eager to pass information on to their visitor. They said they came from a galaxy close by. They had bases on Venus and other planets, including Earth. Their bases on Earth were either underground or beneath the ocean. Their reason for visiting Earth, they told Schirmer, was that "Earth people do not do things in the right way."

Schirmer deduced that their contacts with Earthlings were purely by chance. Fearful they were being seen too often, the aliens wanted to keep people confused.

At one point during their visit one of the beings led Schirmer to a large window in the ship. Pointing to the empty landscape around them, the creature said, "Watchman, someday you will see the Universe!"

After about 15 minutes in the UFO, Schirmer was told that he was not to remember what he had seen. "You will not speak wisely about this night," said one of the creatures. "We will return to see you two more times."

According to investigators, even if Schirmer had wanted to, he could not have reported his extraordinary experience earlier. Before undergoing hypnosis, all he could remember was the first stage of the sighting.

As for the next meetings the beings promised, officer Schirmer is still waiting. ■

*If you have been timed while reading this selection, enter your reading time below. Then turn to the Words-per-Minute table on page 155 and look up your reading speed (words per minute). Enter your reading speed on the graph on page 156.*

READING TIME: Unit 10

_____ : _____
*Minutes        Seconds*

# How well did you read?

- *Answer the four types of questions that follow. The directions for each type of question tell you how to mark your answers.*

- *When you have finished all four exercises, check your work by using the answer key on page 151. For each right answer, put a check mark (✓) on the line beside the box. For each wrong answer, write the correct answer on the line.*

- *For scoring each exercise, follow the directions below the questions.*

## A  FINDING THE MAIN IDEA

Look at the three statements below. One expresses the main idea of the story you just read. A good main idea statement answers two questions: it tells *who* or *what* is the subject of the story, and it answers the understood question *does what?* or *is what?* Another statement is *too broad;* it is vague and doesn't tell much about the topic of the story. The third statement is *too narrow;* it tells about only one part of the story.

Match the statements with the three answer choices below by writing the letter of each answer in the box in front of the statement it goes with.

**M—Main Idea**      **B—Too Broad**      **N—Too Narrow**

____  ☐  1. After officer Schirmer's encounter, he could not account for almost half an hour of his time that evening.

____  ☐  2. Officer Schirmer was not able to recall the details of his UFO encounter until he underwent hypnosis.

____  ☐  3. Officer Schirmer had a UFO encounter.

____  Score 15 points for a correct *M* answer
____  Score 5 points for each correct *B* or *N* answer
____  TOTAL SCORE:  Finding the Main Idea

## B RECALLING FACTS

How well do you remember the facts in the story you just read? Put an *x* in the box in front of the correct answer to each of the multiple-choice questions below.

1. Herbert Schirmer encountered a UFO in
   - ____ ☐ a. Wahoo, Nebraska.
   - ____ ☐ b. Ashland, Nebraska.
   - ____ ☐ c. Omaha, Nebraska.

2. After the encounter officer Schirmer
   - ____ ☐ a. asked to undergo hypnosis.
   - ____ ☐ b. was eager to tell everyone what happened.
   - ____ ☐ c. had trouble sleeping.

3. The spacecraft hovered low over a field because
   - ____ ☐ a. it needed electricity from power lines.
   - ____ ☐ b. the aliens wanted to capture officer Schirmer.
   - ____ ☐ c. the aliens wanted to establish a base on Earth.

4. The aliens on the spacecraft wanted to
   - ____ ☐ a. kill officer Schirmer.
   - ____ ☐ b. take officer Schirmer to Venus.
   - ____ ☐ c. pass along information about themselves.

5. Officer Schirmer remained on the spacecraft for
   - ____ ☐ a. about 15 minutes.
   - ____ ☐ b. over two hours.
   - ____ ☐ c. an unknown length of time.

Score 5 points for each correct answer

____ TOTAL SCORE: Recalling Facts

## C MAKING INFERENCES

An inference is a judgment that is made or an idea that is arrived at based on facts or on information that is given. You make an inference when you understand something that is *not* stated directly but that is *implied*, or suggested, by the facts that are given.

Below are five statements that are judgments or ideas that have been arrived at from the facts of the story. Write the letter *C* in the box in front of each statement that is a correct inference. Write the letter *F* in front of each faulty inference.

**C—Correct Inference    F—Faulty Inference**

- ____ ☐ 1. Nebraska is the site of many UFO sightings.
- ____ ☐ 2. Hypnosis can be a useful tool for helping people to recall events.
- ____ ☐ 3. No one was interested in hearing officer Schirmer's story.
- ____ ☐ 4. The aliens wanted to pass on information to Schirmer.
- ____ ☐ 5. The aliens carefully chose the people that they would talk to.

Score 5 points for each correct answer

____ TOTAL SCORE: Making Inferences

## D USING WORDS PRECISELY

Each of the numbered sentences below contains an underlined word or phrase from the story you have just read. Under the sentence are three definitions. One is a *synonym,* a word that means the same or almost the same thing: *big* and *large.* One is an *antonym,* a word that has the opposite or nearly opposite meaning: *love* and *hate.* One is an unrelated word; it has a completely *different* meaning. Match the definitions with the three answer choices by writing the letter that stands for each answer in the box in front of the definition it goes with.

**S—Synonym    A—Antonym    D—Different**

1. As scanty as the report's details were, they excited the interest of UFO investigators.

____  ☐ a. small

____  ☐ b. plenty

____  ☐ c. not enough

2. What's more, he had a red welt under his left ear that he could not explain.

____  ☐ a. dent

____  ☐ b. stitch

____  ☐ c. lump

3. They also all seem to suffer from lapses of time that they cannot account for.

____  ☐ a. passing away

____  ☐ b. continuous

____  ☐ c. mistakes

4. Their heads were strangely thin and elongated.

____  ☐ a. lengthened

____  ☐ b. continued

____  ☐ c. shortened

5. Schirmer deduced that their [the aliens'] contacts with Earthlings were purely by chance.

____  ☐ a. guessed

____  ☐ b. figured out

____  ☐ c. traced

____  Score 3 points for each correct *S* answer
____  Score 1 point for each correct *A* or *D* answer

____  TOTAL SCORE: Using Words Precisely

● *Enter the four total scores in the spaces below, and add them together to find your Critical Reading Score. Then record your Critical Reading Score on the graph on page 157.*

_____  Finding the Main Idea
_____  Recalling Facts
_____  Making Inferences
_____  Using Words Precisely

_____  CRITICAL READING SCORE: Unit 10

*Heavy rain splashed against the window as Dr. X slowly opened it. He was curious about the flashes of light in the nighttime sky. He probably expected to see lightning. Instead, Dr. X saw two disk-shaped objects with blinking lights hovering in the distance. The objects moved toward him, drawing Dr. X into a puzzling UFO encounter. Investigators still can't explain the strange events.*

# Dr. X Finds a Cure

Some people who report UFO sightings enjoy new-found fame. Yet many more people who encounter UFOs want no publicity. Some even refuse to allow their names to be used in reports. Such is the case of Dr. X, a well-known medical doctor in southern France.

On November 1, 1968, Dr. X awoke about 4:00 A.M. to the sound of his infant son crying. When he reached the child's bedroom, he noticed flashes of light outside the window.

"It's all right, son," soothed the doctor. "It's only lightning."

Although there was no thunder, it was raining very hard. Deciding to make sure that nothing was amiss, the doctor walked through the house, which was built on the side of a hill. The light flashes continued, and seemed to be coming from the west. Opening the large window that led to the terrace, the doctor looked out over the open landscape. Then he spotted them. Two disk-shaped objects hovered in the sky. They were silvery white on top and bright red beneath. Lights were flashing from antennae on top of the disks at about one-second intervals. As the doctor watched in amazement, the objects moved closer to the house. As they did they appeared to merge into a single disk!

The disk continued to draw nearer, a beam of white light beneath it. At first the craft moved horizontally. Then it flipped on its side so that it looked like a discus standing on edge. A beam of light lit the house, shining straight on the doctor's face. At that moment he heard a loud bang. The disk disappeared, leaving a whitish glow that was slowly blown away by the wind.

Badly shaken, the doctor woke up his wife. After he told her about his extraordinary experience, she noticed something that her husband, in his excitement, had overlooked.

"Look at your leg!" she exclaimed. "All the swelling is gone!"

Three days before the doctor had injured his leg while chopping wood. It was so swollen and painful that he had trouble walking. Now, although a slight bruise was still visible, his leg was no longer swollen and the pain had completely disappeared!

The doctor was amazed by how suddenly his injury had healed. But in the days that followed he was to become even more amazed. As a soldier in the war between France and Algeria 10 years earlier, Dr. X had stepped on a land mine. The explosion partially paralyzed the right side of his body. Once a gifted pianist, he could no longer play. He also walked with a pronounced limp. Not long after the UFO sighting, however, he noticed that feeling was returning to his limbs. Soon he was completely cured!

On November 8, six days after the sighting, a UFO investigator named Aimé Michel visited Dr. X. Over the next few years, he closely observed the doctor's case. But on his first meeting with Dr. X, Michel noted that, while the doctor seemed happy to be cured of his ailments, he was quite upset by his experience. He had lost weight and felt very tired. The doctor also suffered from severe cramps and stomach pains. In addition, a peculiar red rash formed a triangle around his navel. Curious about its cause, Dr. X visited a skin specialist. The specialist could find no explanation for the rash or its strange shape.

The day after his exam, Dr. X made an unsettling discovery. The same red triangle had appeared on his son's stomach! For years, the triangle would appear and disappear on both father and son. In fact, in 1986, 18 years after the UFO sighting, the curious red triangles were still quite visible on both the doctor and his son. Investigators even recorded it on film.

Dr. X never had another UFO encounter. But his one experience has had a profound effect on the life of his family. They are more accepting of the world around them. Life and death have a new meaning for them. They have become used to strange events happening around them. They are often able to read each other's minds. The doctor has experienced a phenomenon called levitation; that is, his body rises and floats in the air for no explainable reason! Clocks also start and stop and electrical circuits react oddly when the doctor is near.

The case of Dr. X has been reviewed by many investigators. No one involved doubts that the doctor is telling what he believes to be the truth. But many questions remain unanswered. Did Dr. X's medical cure result from his UFO experience? Is the strange triangle somehow connected to alien visitors? Did the sighting cause Dr. X, his wife, and their son to become more sensitive to events that cannot be explained by modern science? Or is everything that happened to Dr. X and his family simply coincidental?

Whatever the answers, Dr. X is delighted he can once again play his beloved piano. ■

*If you have been timed while reading this selection, enter your reading time below. Then turn to the Words-per-Minute table on page 155 and look up your reading speed (words per minute). Enter your reading speed on the graph on page 156.*

READING TIME: Unit 11

_____ : _____
*Minutes*        *Seconds*

# How well did you read?

- *Answer the four types of questions that follow. The directions for each type of question tell you how to mark your answers.*

- *When you have finished all four exercises, check your work by using the answer key on page 151. For each right answer, put a check mark (✓) on the line beside the box. For each wrong answer, write the correct answer on the line.*

- *For scoring each exercise, follow the directions below the questions.*

## A  FINDING THE MAIN IDEA

Look at the three statements below. One expresses the main idea of the story you just read. A good main idea statement answers two questions: it tells *who* or *what* is the subject of the story, and it answers the understood question *does what?* or *is what?* Another statement is *too broad;* it is vague and doesn't tell much about the topic of the story. The third statement is *too narrow;* it tells about only one part of the story.

Match the statements with the three answer choices below by writing the letter of each answer in the box in front of the statement it goes with.

**M—Main Idea      B—Too Broad      N—Too Narrow**

_____  ☐  1. After a 1968 encounter with a UFO in France, Dr. X was cured of several physical ailments.

_____  ☐  2. On November 1, 1968, at 4:00 A.M. Dr. X experienced a UFO sighting in France.

_____  ☐  3. Dr. X had several unexplainable experiences.

_____  Score 15 points for a correct *M* answer
_____  Score 5 points for each correct *B* or *N* answer

_____  TOTAL SCORE:  Finding the Main Idea

## B  RECALLING FACTS

How well do you remember the facts in the story you just read? Put an *x* in the box in front of the correct answer to each of the multiple-choice questions below.

1. Dr. X experienced the sighting
   - ____ ☐ a. along with his son.
   - ____ ☐ b. with his wife.
   - ____ ☐ c. alone.

2. At the time of the sighting the weather was
   - ____ ☐ a. cold and windy.
   - ____ ☐ b. rainy.
   - ____ ☐ c. snowy.

3. After the sighting Dr. X
   - ____ ☐ a. tried to calm his son.
   - ____ ☐ b. woke his wife.
   - ____ ☐ c. recorded his thoughts in his diary.

4. Dr. X's paralysis began to get better
   - ____ ☐ a. soon after the sighting.
   - ____ ☐ b. during the sighting.
   - ____ ☐ c. before the sighting.

5. Dr. X's sighting has been investigated by
   - ____ ☐ a. his wife and family.
   - ____ ☐ b. a few close friends.
   - ____ ☐ c. UFO investigators.

Score 5 points for each correct answer

____ TOTAL SCORE: Recalling Facts

## C  MAKING INFERENCES

An inference is a judgment that is made or an idea that is arrived at based on facts or on information that is given. You make an inference when you understand something that is *not* stated directly but that is *implied*, or suggested, by the facts that are given.

Below are five statements that are judgments or ideas that have been arrived at from the facts of the story. Write the letter *C* in the box in front of each statement that is a correct inference. Write the letter *F* in front of each faulty inference.

**C—Correct Inference**     **F—Faulty Inference**

- ____ ☐ 1. Dr. X's son was afraid of the sighting.
- ____ ☐ 2. Dr. X would not allow his name to be used on any reports.
- ____ ☐ 3. The weather was unusual on the night that Dr. X saw the UFO.
- ____ ☐ 4. The sighting had little effect on Dr. X or his family.
- ____ ☐ 5. Dr. X had mixed emotions about his experience.

Score 5 points for each correct answer

____ TOTAL SCORE: Making Inferences

## D  USING WORDS PRECISELY

Each of the numbered sentences below contains an underlined word or phrase from the story you have just read. Under the sentence are three definitions. One is a *synonym*, a word that means the same or almost the same thing: *big* and *large*. One is an *antonym*, a word that has the opposite or nearly opposite meaning: *love* and *hate*. One is an unrelated word; it has a completely *different* meaning. Match the definitions with the three answer choices by writing the letter that stands for each answer in the box in front of the definition it goes with.

**S—Synonym     A—Antonym     D—Different**

1. Deciding to make sure that nothing was <u>amiss</u>, the doctor walked through the house. . . .

____ ☐ a. imperfect

____ ☐ b. out of place

____ ☐ c. in correct order

2. Lights were flashing from antennae on top of the disks at about one-second <u>intervals</u>.

____ ☐ a. divides

____ ☐ b. nonstop or continuous

____ ☐ c. time or spaces between

3. As they did they appeared to <u>merge</u> into a single disk!

____ ☐ a. mix

____ ☐ b. combine

____ ☐ c. separate

4. He also walked with a <u>pronounced</u> limp.

____ ☐ a. unnoticeable

____ ☐ b. declared

____ ☐ c. strongly marked

5. But his one experience has had a <u>profound</u> effect on the life of his family.

____ ☐ a. deeply felt

____ ☐ b. easily understood

____ ☐ c. positive

____ Score 3 points for each correct *S* answer

____ Score 1 point for each correct *A* or *D* answer

____ TOTAL SCORE: Using Words Precisely

● *Enter the four total scores in the spaces below, and add them together to find your Critical Reading Score. Then record your Critical Reading Score on the graph on page 157.*

| | |
|---|---|
| _____ | Finding the Main Idea |
| _____ | Recalling Facts |
| _____ | Making Inferences |
| _____ | Using Words Precisely |
| _____ | CRITICAL READING SCORE: Unit 11 |

The Johnsons of Delphos, Kansas, won $5,000 from the **National Enquirer** for their extraordinary story. In November 1971 they claimed a UFO landed on their farm, leaving behind glowing trees and a ring of white powder. Ronnie Johnson, age 16, saw the UFO first. The Johnsons' story made them famous, but not everyone believed they were telling the truth.

# The Delphos Ring

What is supposed to have happened on the Johnson farm in Delphos, Kansas, could have been a hoax. Several aspects of the 1971 case did seem suspicious. Many investigators doubt the Johnsons' story; however, no one has ever completely proved or disproved the family's claim that the strange white ring on the ground near their farmhouse was left by a mushroom-shaped UFO.

At 7:00 in the evening of November 2, 1971, 16-year-old Ronnie Johnson was tending sheep in a field near his house when he heard an ominous rumbling sound. Suddenly an object shaped like a mushroom appeared about 25 yards away. Lit all over by multicolored lights, it hovered close to the ground, making a sound like "an old washing machine that vibrates." A single shaft of white light under the object beamed toward the ground. Ronnie stood in awe, paralyzed and blinded by the brilliance, until the object suddenly flew away toward the town of Delphos.

It took about 15 minutes for Ronnie's eyes to recover from the blinding light. Then he burst into the house to tell his parents. Reluctantly, Erma and Durel Johnson followed their son outside. It was obvious to Ronnie that they did not believe him. But the object was still visible high in the sky. The three witnesses watched as the UFO, which Erma Johnson described as looking "like a giant washtub," moved toward the south and disappeared.

No longer skeptical, the Johnsons followed their son to the grove of trees where the object had hovered. They claimed that some of the trees were glowing, and on the ground a circle glowed with the same gray-white light. When they touched the soil, which appeared to have been dusted with a white powder, it seemed to have a strange texture. Erma Johnson later said that her fingertips became numb. A nurse at a local hospital, she was unable to take the pulse of her patients for two weeks after the event. Durel Johnson also reported numbness in his fingers, although his condition soon disappeared.

Erma Johnson took photographs of the ring while her husband and son drove into Delphos. They went straight to the local newspaper offices.

The next day a news reporter visited the Johnson farm. She studied Mrs. Johnson's Polaroid photograph, which showed the glowing ring. Testing the circle of soil, the reporter noted that it felt dry and crusted and was lighter in color than the surrounding soil, which was quite muddy. Mrs. Johnson pointed out a dead tree that had been knocked down, she said, by the UFO.

Once the story hit the news wires, investigators came to the Johnson farm in droves. One of these, Ted Phillips, arrived about a month later after a snowfall. Phillips reported that snow was melting both outside and inside the ring, but the one-foot-wide ring was perfectly white.

"We removed snow from one section of the ring and introduced water into the exposed ring area," the report stated. "The soil would not permit the water to pass through the surface. This was most remarkable, as there had been several inches of rain and snow."

After taking a sample from the ring, Phillips noted that the soil under the ring was dry to a depth of at least one foot.

Later studies of soil samples from the ring revealed that it contained a fungus called fairy ring mushroom, which may glow under certain conditions. There is no evidence that the fungus was produced in outer space.

Another investigator, Philip Klass, pointed out several problems with the Johnsons' story.

Why had the Johnsons reported their claim to the local newspaper instead of the police? As a result they were now enjoying greatly the attention and fame their report had brought them.

If they had been paralyzed by the white powder in the ring, why hadn't the Johnsons been to a doctor? Other people who had handled the powder, including the local sheriff, had not experienced any numbness.

Why did the Johnsons refuse to take a lie detector test?

The dead tree also raised some questions. If the UFO had come from the south and taken off toward the south, as Ronnie had reported, the tree would have fallen in a different direction. The tree also had no marks showing where it had supposedly been struck.

Erma Johnson claimed that her Polaroid photographs were taken at night with only the glow from the UFO for light. But only one picture showed a glow, and it was orange. What's more, it lit the side of a tree trunk farthest from the ring. The Johnsons finally admitted that a sunset might have caused the glow. When an expert analyzed the picture of the ring itself, the photographer concluded that the picture had been taken using a flashbulb.

But not everyone was as skeptical of the Johnsons' story. In 1972 the *National Enquirer* newspaper offered a $50,000 prize to anyone who could prove that a spaceship from another planet had visited Earth. Although the five judges concluded that none of the more than 1,000 entries qualified for the top prize, they awarded $5,000 to the Johnsons of Delphos, Kansas.

Experienced with UFO cases, the judges were impressed with details of the Johnsons' story that matched those in other UFO landings. Both Ronnie Johnson and his dog were rooted to the spot during the sighting itself. For about two weeks after the sighting, every sunset, the sheep on the farm began to act in a bizarre manner, jumping out of the pen and running around wildly for a time. When it started to grow dark, the dog tried frantically to get into the house, eventually destroying the screen door. Like some other UFO witnesses, Ronnie Johnson suffered from eye problems for days after the event. He also had headaches and nightmares. He would wake up screaming after dreaming that humanlike creatures were looking into his bedroom window. The judges also noted that the ring-shaped pattern on the Johnson farm was similar to those in hundreds of other supposed UFO sightings around the world.

Whether or not the Johnsons' story is a true UFO encounter is still under debate. ■

*If you have been timed while reading this selection, enter your reading time below. Then turn to the Words-per-Minute table on page 155 and look up your reading speed (words per minute). Enter your reading speed on the graph on page 156.*

| READING TIME: Unit 12 |
| --- |
| _____ : _____ |
| *Minutes*   *Seconds* |

# How well did you read?

- *Answer the four types of questions that follow. The directions for each type of question tell you how to mark your answers.*

- *When you have finished all four exercises, check your work by using the answer key on page 151. For each right answer, put a check mark (✓) on the line beside the box. For each wrong answer, write the correct answer on the line.*

- *For scoring each exercise, follow the directions below the questions.*

## A  FINDING THE MAIN IDEA

Look at the three statements below. One expresses the main idea of the story you just read. A good main idea statement answers two questions: it tells *who* or *what* is the subject of the story, and it answers the understood question *does what?* or *is what?* Another statement is *too broad;* it is vague and doesn't tell much about the topic of the story. The third statement is *too narrow;* it tells about only one part of the story.

  Match the statements with the three answer choices below by writing the letter of each answer in the box in front of the statement it goes with.

**M—Main Idea**      **B—Too Broad**      **N—Too Narrow**

_____ ☐ 1. Over the years there have been many reported UFO sightings that investigators doubt actually happened.

_____ ☐ 2. Ronnie Johnson was temporarily paralyzed and blinded by the UFO.

_____ ☐ 3. The Johnson family claims to have encountered a UFO in November 1971, though many experts believe it was a hoax.

_____ Score 15 points for a correct *M* answer

_____ Score 5 points for each correct *B* or *N* answer

_____ TOTAL SCORE: Finding the Main Idea

## B  RECALLING FACTS

How well do you remember the facts in the story you just read? Put an *x* in the box in front of the correct answer to each of the multiple-choice questions below.

1. The Johnsons' encounter took place in
   - ____ ☐ a. Missouri.
   - ____ ☐ b. Nebraska.
   - ____ ☐ c. Kansas.

2. The Johnson who first saw the UFO was
   - ____ ☐ a. Durel, the father.
   - ____ ☐ b. Erma, the mother.
   - ____ ☐ c. Ronnie, the son.

3. To Erma the UFO looked like a
   - ____ ☐ a. mushroom.
   - ____ ☐ b. giant washtub.
   - ____ ☐ c. old washing machine.

4. The Johnsons first reported their sighting to the
   - ____ ☐ a. hospital.
   - ____ ☐ b. police.
   - ____ ☐ c. local newspaper.

5. Erma Johnson worked as a
   - ____ ☐ a. farmer.
   - ____ ☐ b. nurse.
   - ____ ☐ c. newspaper reporter.

Score 5 points for each correct answer

____ TOTAL SCORE:  Recalling Facts

## C  MAKING INFERENCES

An inference is a judgment that is made or an idea that is arrived at based on facts or on information that is given. You make an inference when you understand something that is *not* stated directly but that is *implied*, or suggested, by the facts that are given.

Below are five statements that are judgments or ideas that have been arrived at from the facts of the story. Write the letter *C* in the box in front of each statement that is a correct inference. Write the letter *F* in front of each faulty inference.

**C—Correct Inference**     **F—Faulty Inference**

- ____ ☐ 1. Sixteen-year-old Ronnie enjoyed farming.
- ____ ☐ 2. Ronnie was affected deeply by his experience.
- ____ ☐ 3. That the Johnsons won a prize for their story suggests strongly they were telling the truth.
- ____ ☐ 4. The Johnsons probably made up their story so that they could make a lot of money.
- ____ ☐ 5. A satisfactory answer to the Johnsons' story may never be found.

Score 5 points for each correct answer

____ TOTAL SCORE:  Making Inferences

## D  USING WORDS PRECISELY

Each of the numbered sentences below contains an underlined word or phrase from the story you have just read. Under the sentence are three definitions. One is a *synonym*, a word that means the same or almost the same thing: *big* and *large*. One is an *antonym*, a word that has the opposite or nearly opposite meaning: *love* and *hate*. One is an unrelated word; it has a completely *different* meaning. Match the definitions with the three answer choices by writing the letter that stands for each answer in the box in front of the definition it goes with.

**S—Synonym     A—Antonym     D—Different**

1. Several <u>aspects</u> of the 1971 case did seem suspicious.

____ ☐ a. facts

____ ☐ b. thoughts or views

____ ☐ c. position of planets

2. . . . Ronnie Johnson was tending sheep in a field near his house when he heard an <u>ominous</u> sound.

____ ☐ a. unlucky

____ ☐ b. threatening

____ ☐ c. harmless

3. A single <u>shaft</u> of white light under the object beamed toward the ground.

____ ☐ a. ray or beam

____ ☐ b. floodlight

____ ☐ c. passageway

4. Ronnie stood in <u>awe</u>, paralyzed and blinded by the brilliance. . . .

____ ☐ a. panic

____ ☐ b. calmness

____ ☐ c. fear

5. No longer <u>skeptical</u>, the Johnsons followed their son to the grove of trees where the object had hovered.

____ ☐ a. doubting

____ ☐ b. confused

____ ☐ c. certain

____ Score 3 points for each correct *S* answer
____ Score 1 point for each correct *A* or *D* answer

____ TOTAL SCORE: Using Words Precisely

● *Enter the four total scores in the spaces below, and add them together to find your Critical Reading Score. Then record your Critical Reading Score on the graph on page 157.*

_____ Finding the Main Idea
_____ Recalling Facts
_____ Making Inferences
_____ Using Words Precisely

_____ CRITICAL READING SCORE:  Unit 12

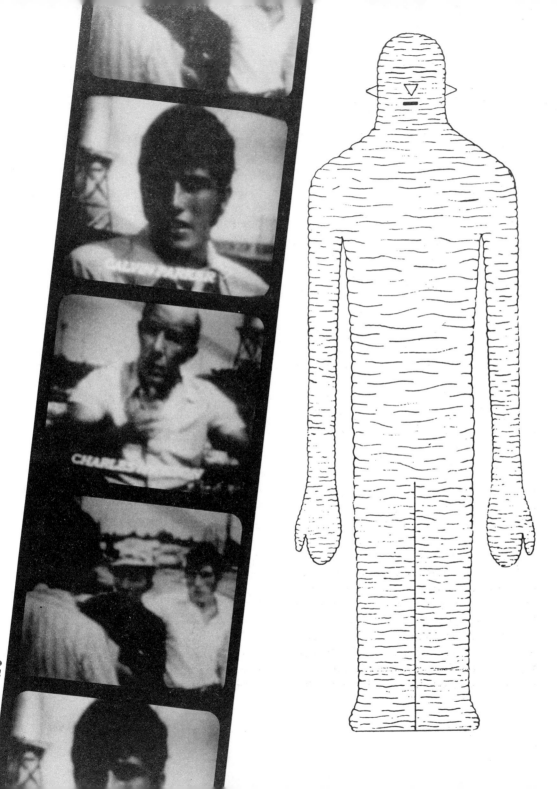

*What would you do if you saw this alien creature? Calvin Parker says he passed out, and Charles Hickson claims he tried to run away. Both men were clearly frightened when they told the Pascagoula, Mississippi, sheriff about their UFO encounter. The sheriff didn't think it was a hoax. Parker and Hickson repeated their story on television and became instant celebrities. Were they out to make money?*

# The Pascagoula Encounter

Despite the difference in their ages, Calvin Parker, age 19, and Charles Hickson, age 42, enjoyed each other's company. After a long day at the shipyard where they both worked, the men often spent the evening fishing in the Pascagoula River. But those days are long gone. Now Hickson and Parker say they are too afraid to fish there. What happened on that warm Mississippi night might happen again.

It was early in the evening on October 11, 1973. The men had been fishing for about an hour when they noticed a blue light coming at them through the darkness.

Parker's heart nearly jumped out of his chest. "What's that?" he screamed as the thing came closer, making an odd buzzing sound.

Hickson had no answer. He stared in amazement as the object came within 30 yards of him. Hovering only a few feet above the water was a glowing oblong craft about 20 or 30 feet long.

Suddenly a door in the side of the craft opened and three weird-looking creatures floated toward the men. Hickson and Parker stood petrified. As Hickson later stated, " . . . I started to hit the river, man. And Calvin just—he went hysterical."

The creatures were average in height, about five feet tall, with bulletlike heads and no necks. They were covered with grayish, wrinkled skin, which Hickson described as like "the skin of an elephant." They had slits for mouths and thin, cone-shaped appendages instead of noses and ears. Strangely, they seemed to have no eyes. The creatures had two arms that ended in lobsterlike pincers. Although they had what looked like two legs, the legs seemed to be connected and ended in round-shaped feet.

Too terrified to run, Hickson and Parker stood rooted as the creatures floated toward them, making strange buzzing noises. Before he knew what was happening, two of the aliens grabbed Hickson under the arms and began lifting him toward the craft. When the third creature grabbed Parker, the young man passed out.

Inside the spaceship Hickson recalls being taken to a brightly lighted room where he was examined with a machine. "It looked like a big eye," Hickson said, "and it went all over my body, up and down." When the exam was over, Hickson's body was left hanging in midair. He could not move a muscle.

After 15 or 20 minutes Hickson was floated out of the ship and back to the ground where Parker sat, crying. The two men watched the UFO rise straight up and out of sight.

Unharmed but badly frightened, Hickson and Parker debated what to do. Should they report what had happened? At first they decided to keep quiet. After all, who would believe their incredible story? But then, thinking the government should know about what had happened, they decided to tell their story to the local sheriff.

Four hours after their experience, Hickson and Parker were interviewed by Sheriff Fred Diamond and Captain Glen Ryder at the Pascagoula sheriff's office. Every word was tape recorded. Unknown to Hickson and Parker, however, the tape recorder was left running when the two men were left alone. Hickson's voice trembled a bit, while Parker still sounded frantic.

"I passed out. I expect I never passed out in my whole life," said Parker.

"I've never seen nothin' like that before in my life," said Hickson. "They won't believe it. They gonna believe it one of these days. Might be too late. I knew all along they was people from other worlds up there. I knew all along. I never thought it would happen to me."

Listening to the tape, the sheriff was impressed. This didn't sound like a hoax. Asked later if he believed the statements made by Hickson and Parker, Sheriff Diamond replied: "First thing they wanted to do was take a lie detector test. Charlie—he was shook bad." The sheriff added that you don't see a man like Hickson "break down and cry from excitement unless it's something fierce happened."

The day after their encounter local newspapers ran Hickson's and Parker's stories, and in a few days it became nationwide news. Investigators thronged to Pascagoula. Charles Hickson and Calvin Parker were overnight celebrities.

Unlike many UFO victims, Hickson and Parker had total recall of their encounter. Still they both agreed to be hypnotized. One of those present at the sessions was Dr. J. Allen Hynek. He said later: "There's simply no question in my mind that these men have had a very real frightening experience. . . . They are absolutely honest." Dr. James Harder agreed. "The experience they underwent was indeed a real one," he said. "A very strong feeling of terror is practically impossible to fake under hypnosis."

Yet there were skeptics. Had Hickson and Parker invented their story to make money? It was pointed out that Hickson, fired from his last job for "unsuitable" conduct, needed money, even though he was reemployed at the time of the incident.

There had also been a bridge attendant who had been on duty near the pier where Hickson and Parker had been fishing that evening. He claimed that he saw nothing unusual that night.

As further proof of their claim, Hickson and Parker agreed to take a lie detector test. Hickson passed with flying colors. However, Parker suffered a nervous breakdown and never did take the test.

Still unsatisfied, critics pointed out that lie detectors are not infallible. And, they asked, why didn't Hickson take the test locally? Instead, he traveled all the way to New Orleans, Louisiana, where the operator was picked by Hickson's lawyer. And the operator, according to some investigators, was not fully qualified to administer lie detector tests. Despite the critics, Hickson declined to take the test again.

No one has ever been able to prove conclusively that the Pascagoula encounter was a hoax. And Charles Hickson still insists the event happened just as he described it. But Philip Klass, an investigator who

reviewed the case, suspects that it is a hoax. He feels there are too many discrepancies in Hickson's account.

Interviewed in 1987, Hickson said, "I make my living with my hands. I had a chance to make a million dollars . . . back in 1973. I was offered all kinds of money to let them do a movie. I declined. I am still declining. Making money is not what this experience is about." Yet Hickson gave up his job and made appearances on national television after the supposed encounter. ■

*If you have been timed while reading this selection, enter your reading time below. Then turn to the Words-per-Minute table on page 155 and look up your reading speed (words per minute). Enter your reading speed on the graph on page 156.*

READING TIME: Unit 13

—————— : ——————
*Minutes*      *Seconds*

# How well did you read?

- *Answer the four types of questions that follow. The directions for each type of question tell you how to mark your answers.*

- *When you have finished all four exercises, check your work by using the answer key on page 151. For each right answer, put a check mark (✓) on the line beside the box. For each wrong answer, write the correct answer on the line.*

- *For scoring each exercise, follow the directions below the questions.*

## A  FINDING THE MAIN IDEA

Look at the three statements below. One expresses the main idea of the story you just read. A good main idea statement answers two questions: it tells *who* or *what* is the subject of the story, and it answers the understood question *does what?* or *is what?* Another statement is *too broad;* it is vague and doesn't tell much about the topic of the story. The third statement is *too narrow;* it tells about only one part of the story.

Match the statements with the three answer choices below by writing the letter of each answer in the box in front of the statement it goes with.

**M—Main Idea      B—Too Broad      N—Too Narrow**

____ ☐ 1. Two friends from Pascagoula, Mississippi, who reportedly encountered aliens from outer space, had trouble convincing everyone that their story was true.

____ ☐ 2. It's not always easy to prove that some UFO encounters are hoaxes.

____ ☐ 3. Hickson took a lie detector test to prove his story about an encounter with aliens from outer space, but his friend, Calvin Parker, did not.

____ Score 15 points for a correct *M* answer

____ Score 5 points for each correct *B* or *N* answer

____ TOTAL SCORE:  Finding the Main Idea

## B  RECALLING FACTS

How well do you remember the facts in the story you just read?
Put an *x* in the box in front of the correct answer to each of the
multiple-choice questions below.

1. Calvin Parker and Charles Hickson
   - ___ ☐ a. were about the same age.
   - ___ ☐ b. were cousins.
   - ___ ☐ c. had a large difference in their ages.

2. The creatures that Calvin and Charles encountered were
   - ___ ☐ a. average in height.
   - ___ ☐ b. quite tall.
   - ___ ☐ c. tall and quite humanlike.

3. When the creatures approached them, Calvin and Charles
   - ___ ☐ a. were too terrified to run.
   - ___ ☐ b. were eager to greet them.
   - ___ ☐ c. laughed, assuming it was a hoax.

4. The event left Calvin and Charles
   - ___ ☐ a. happy.
   - ___ ☐ b. confused and angry.
   - ___ ☐ c. unharmed but badly frightened.

5. As a result of the encounter, Calvin and Charles became
   - ___ ☐ a. even closer friends.
   - ___ ☐ b. enemies.
   - ___ ☐ c. overnight celebrities.

Score 5 points for each correct answer

___ TOTAL SCORE:  Recalling Facts

## C  MAKING INFERENCES

An inference is a judgment that is made or an idea that is arrived
at based on facts or on information that is given. You make an
inference when you understand something that is *not* stated
directly but that is *implied,* or suggested, by the facts that are given.

Below are five statements that are judgments or ideas that have
been arrived at from the facts of the story. Write the letter *C* in
the box in front of each statement that is a correct inference. Write
the letter *F* in front of each faulty inference.

**C—Correct Inference      F—Faulty Inference**

- ___ ☐ 1. Even though people may have a big difference in their ages, they can still be friends.

- ___ ☐ 2. Calvin Parker thought of Charles Hickson as his father.

- ___ ☐ 3. The police didn't care whether or not the two men were telling the truth.

- ___ ☐ 4. Parker and Hickson recalled their encounter even before they were hypnotized.

- ___ ☐ 5. Charles Hickson's life did not change at all after the encounter.

Score 5 points for each correct answer

___ TOTAL SCORE:  Making Inferences

## D USING WORDS PRECISELY

Each of the numbered sentences below contains an underlined word or phrase from the story you have just read. Under the sentence are three definitions. One is a *synonym*, a word that means the same or almost the same thing: *big* and *large*. One is an *antonym*, a word that has the opposite or nearly opposite meaning: *love* and *hate*. One is an unrelated word; it has a completely *different* meaning. Match the definitions with the three answer choices by writing the letter that stands for each answer in the box in front of the definition it goes with.

**S—Synonym      A—Antonym      D—Different**

1. Hickson and Parker stood <u>petrified</u>.

___ ☐ a. made bold

___ ☐ b. changed into stone

___ ☐ c. made motionless by fear

2. They had slits for mouths and thin, cone-shaped <u>appendages</u> instead of noses and ears.

___ ☐ a. attached parts

___ ☐ b. separate parts

___ ☐ c. additions

3. Hickson passed [the lie detector test] with <u>flying colors</u>.

___ ☐ a. just passed

___ ☐ b. failed miserably

___ ☐ c. completely successful

4. No one has ever been able to prove <u>conclusively</u> that the Pascagoula encounter was a hoax.

___ ☐ a. without a doubt

___ ☐ b. doubtful

___ ☐ c. arranged

5. He [the investigator] feels there are too many <u>discrepancies</u> in Hickson's account.

___ ☐ a. similarities

___ ☐ b. differences

___ ☐ c. arguments

___ Score 3 points for each correct *S* answer
___ Score 1 point for each correct *A* or *D* answer

___ TOTAL SCORE: Using Words Precisely

● *Enter the four total scores in the spaces below, and add them together to find your Critical Reading Score. Then record your Critical Reading Score on the graph on page 157.*

_____ Finding the Main Idea
_____ Recalling Facts
_____ Making Inferences
_____ Using Words Precisely
_____ CRITICAL READING SCORE: Unit 13

Ian and Susan Blackwell (not their real names) thought they'd have a peaceful drive to Durban, South Africa. That is, until an eerie glow surrounded their car! Ian suspected the glow was from a UFO, and when he lost control of the car, he knew his suspicion was dead right. He would later learn from hypnosis that he had quite an adventure on board the spacecraft.

# The Beit Bridge Encounter

Spotting what he thought was a speed trap on the road ahead, Ian Blackwell (not his real name) eased his foot off the accelerator of his Peugeot 404. He didn't need a speeding ticket at this hour of the night—or any hour, for that matter!

"That sure is an odd-looking uniform," said his wife, Susan, as they passed what she thought was a police officer.

"It looks like he's wearing a plastic or metal suit," agreed Ian. But when he glanced back in the rearview mirror, the oddly dressed "policeman" had disappeared.

Breathing a sigh of relief, Ian picked up speed once again. Susan continued to stare out the car window into the surrounding blackness. Except for an infrequent farm town, there was little to see in this part of Africa but dry, desolate scrublands. It was 2:30 A.M. on May 30, 1974. Soon they would reach the Limpopo River, which borders the countries of Zimbabwe (then known as Rhodesia) and South Africa. After crossing the Beit Bridge, they would head for the city of Durban on the South African coast.

As Susan fought off sleep, she noticed a light off to the left side of their car that seemed to be keeping pace with them. No sooner had she pointed out the light to her husband than their own car lights faded, and an eerie glow surrounded them. The warm night air suddenly grew very cold.

"Ian, what's happening?" cried Susan.

Shivering from the cold, the Blackwells bundled in coats and blankets. Ian checked the car's electrical equipment and was relieved to find that except for the headlights, everything seemed to be in working order.

"I don't know what's happening, but I do know we're getting out of here," he answered. Ian did not want to reveal his apprehension: they were being followed by a UFO!

Glancing at the speedometer, Ian realized he was traveling at close to 90 miles per hour. But when he took his foot off the accelerator, instead of slowing down the car continued to speed ahead, as if it had a mind of its own! Ian desperately tried to stop the car, but it was completely out of his control. Terrified, he stared at the road, not saying a word to Susan.

After speeding along for 11 miles the Blackwells reached a gas station in the town of Fort Victoria. By this time it was 4:30 in the morning, and the strange light had disappeared. Still cold, Ian and Susan were surprised to see the attendant at the station dressed only in shorts. When they resumed their drive, they were relieved that the strange light seemed to have disappeared.

But about six miles outside town the light appeared again on the left side of the car. Another light was positioned directly overhead. Although the Blackwells had

expected a lot of traffic on the road from Fort Victoria to Beit Bridge, since many people time their trips to avoid driving in the daytime heat, the road was deserted. The lack of traffic was all the more surprising because the previous day had been a public holiday.

As he drove, Ian began to wonder if he had possibly taken the wrong road. The terrain was an unexpected mixture of low bushes, high grass, marshes, and swamps. The road itself, normally very curved and twisted, was perfectly straight. And there was an eerie silence around them: the car engine made no noise; there was no rustling and buzzing of insects. Once again Ian lost control of the car. Although they were traveling at about 125 miles per hour, "I wasn't driving," Ian recalled. Still, he stayed nervously awake while Susan fell asleep.

When they finally arrived at Beit Bridge it was light enough to make out two UFOs hovering high above them. The clock at Zimbabwe customs showed 8:30 A.M. But the car clock and Ian's and Susan's watches all read 7:30 A.M. What had happened to the lost hour?

Ian was in for an even bigger surprise when he checked the car's mileage. The distance between Fort Victoria and Beit Bridge is approximately 179 miles. However, the trip meter registered only 10½ miles! And the gas tank, which should have been nearly empty from the trip, took only 22 cents worth of gasoline!

Could there be some logical explanation? Frightened and confused, the Blackwells decided to report the strange events to UFO investigators.

Clearly, something incredible had taken place on the Blackwells' journey to Beit Bridge. Investigators found the Peugeot's tires especially puzzling. To save money, Ian had bought inexpensive retreads for the trip, knowing that good tires would be available at a reasonable cost in South Africa. He figured that the retreads would be good for about 750 miles. However, when Ian showed the tires to investigators, the car had traveled nearly 5,000 miles—and the retreads still looked brand new!

Hoping to find out what had happened on their trip, the Blackwells agreed to undergo hypnosis. Only then did the whole story unfold. When Susan had fallen asleep on the road to Beit Bridge, Ian recalled that a "space being" had been projected into the car's rear seat. The being could take any form that Ian imagined; if Ian imagined a tree, that is what the being would look like!

Ian also toured the spacecraft, although somehow his physical body never left the car. Was it an out-of-body experience? Approximately 90 feet wide and 60 feet high, the spacecraft had three levels. These included a flight deck and areas for engineering, communications, and living quarters. There was also a special area where abducted humans were taken—an empty room that could somehow simulate earthly surroundings.

Ian learned that while the beings had a physical form, they traveled in time rather than space. They made frequent trips to Earth and even lived among humans as ordinary-looking people! The purpose of their contact, they explained, was to influence future events on Earth without becoming directly involved.

When Ian "returned" to his car, he had no memory of what had taken place. Susan continued to sleep as they drove on to Beit Bridge, their persistent escorts hovering overhead. But after the Peugeot crossed the border the UFOs disappeared, leaving the Blackwells to enjoy an uneventful trip to the South African coast.

Like many others who claim to have had a UFO encounter, the Blackwells prefer to remain anonymous. Despite their extraordinary experience, they want to live ordinary lives. But in the back of their minds there is always the nagging fear that what happened on the road to Beit Bridge might happen again. ■

*If you have been timed while reading this selection, enter your reading time below. Then turn to the Words-per-Minute table on page 155 and look up your reading speed (words per minute). Enter your reading speed on the graph on page 156.*

READING TIME: Unit 14

_____ : _____
Minutes          Seconds

# How well did you read?

- *Answer the four types of questions that follow. The directions for each type of question tell you how to mark your answers.*

- *When you have finished all four exercises, check your work by using the answer key on page 151. For each right answer, put a check mark (✓) on the line beside the box. For each wrong answer, write the correct answer on the line.*

- *For scoring each exercise, follow the directions below the questions.*

## A  FINDING THE MAIN IDEA

Look at the three statements below. One expresses the main idea of the story you just read. A good main idea statement answers two questions: it tells *who* or *what* is the subject of the story, and it answers the understood question *does what?* or *is what?* Another statement is *too broad;* it is vague and doesn't tell much about the topic of the story. The third statement is *too narrow;* it tells about only one part of the story.

Match the statements with the three answer choices below by writing the letter of each answer in the box in front of the statement it goes with.

**M—Main Idea      B—Too Broad      N—Too Narrow**

_____ ☐ 1. The Blackwells' UFO encounter in South Africa left them afraid and confused.

_____ ☐ 2. On their way to Beit Bridge the Blackwells noticed an eerie glow surrounding their car.

_____ ☐ 3. Many people who claim to have seen UFOs want to remain anonymous.

_____ Score 15 points for a correct *M* answer

_____ Score 5 points for each correct *B* or *N* answer

_____ TOTAL SCORE: Finding the Main Idea

## B RECALLING FACTS

How well do you remember the facts in the story you just read?
Put an *x* in the box in front of the correct answer to each of the
multiple-choice questions below.

1. The couple in the story do not want to be identified
   because they
   - ___ ☐ a. are shy.
   - ___ ☐ b. want to go on living a normal life.
   - ___ ☐ c. are afraid the aliens will track them down
           if they use their real names.

2. On the night of the encounter, the Blackwells were
   traveling to
   - ___ ☐ a. Durban, South Africa.
   - ___ ☐ b. Fort Victoria.
   - ___ ☐ c. Zimbabwe.

3. At one point in their journey, Ian wondered if they
   - ___ ☐ a. might be killed.
   - ___ ☐ b. might be lost.
   - ___ ☐ c. would find an open gas station.

4. Ian recalled that the space being in the back seat of the car
   - ___ ☐ a. looked like a bush.
   - ___ ☐ b. could assume many different forms.
   - ___ ☐ c. would cause Susan to panic.

5. Hoping to find out what really happened, the Blackwells
   - ___ ☐ a. talked about their experience with friends.
   - ___ ☐ b. went to the police.
   - ___ ☐ c. agreed to undergo hypnosis.

Score 5 points for each correct answer

___ TOTAL SCORE: Recalling Facts

## C MAKING INFERENCES

An inference is a judgment that is made or an idea that is arrived
at based on facts or on information that is given. You make an
inference when you understand something that is *not* stated
directly but that is *implied,* or suggested, by the facts that are given.

Below are five statements that are judgments or ideas that have
been arrived at from the facts of the story. Write the letter C in
the box in front of each statement that is a correct inference. Write
the letter *F* in front of each faulty inference.

**C—Correct Inference      F—Faulty Inference**

- ___ ☐ 1. Ian Blackwell was a thrifty man.
- ___ ☐ 2. The aliens were afraid of people on Earth.
- ___ ☐ 3. Susan Blackwell knew her husband went aboard
           the spacecraft.
- ___ ☐ 4. People don't travel much the day after a public
           holiday in South Africa.
- ___ ☐ 5. The Blackwells will always fear strange lights
           at night.

Score 5 points for each correct answer

___ TOTAL SCORE: Making Inferences

## D USING WORDS PRECISELY

Each of the numbered sentences below contains an underlined word or phrase from the story you have just read. Under the sentence are three definitions. One is a *synonym,* a word that means the same or almost the same thing: *big* and *large.* One is an *antonym,* a word that has the opposite or nearly opposite meaning: *love* and *hate.* One is an unrelated word; it has a completely *different* meaning. Match the definitions with the three answer choices by writing the letter that stands for each answer in the box in front of the definition it goes with.

**S—Synonym      A—Antonym      D—Different**

1. Ian did not want to reveal his <u>apprehension</u>: they were being followed by a UFO!

____ ☐ a. awe

____ ☐ b. fear

____ ☐ c. confidence

2. And there was an eerie silence . . . there was no <u>rustling</u> and buzzing of insects.

____ ☐ a. murmuring

____ ☐ b. moving loudly

____ ☐ c. gathering

3. . . . Ian recalled that a "space being" had been <u>projected</u> into the car's rear seat.

____ ☐ a. vanished

____ ☐ b. thrown forward

____ ☐ c. appeared

4. There was also a special area . . . an empty room that could somehow <u>simulate</u> earthly surroundings.

____ ☐ a. imitate

____ ☐ b. pretend

____ ☐ c. disguise

5. Susan continued to sleep as they drove on to Beit Bridge, their <u>persistent</u> escorts hovering overhead.

____ ☐ a. stubborn

____ ☐ b. occasional

____ ☐ c. constant

____ Score 3 points for each correct *S* answer

____ Score 1 point for each correct *A* or *D* answer

____ TOTAL SCORE: Using Words Precisely

● *Enter the four total scores in the spaces below, and add them together to find your Critical Reading Score. Then record your Critical Reading Score on the graph on page 157.*

_____ Finding the Main Idea
_____ Recalling Facts
_____ Making Inferences
_____ Using Words Precisely
_____ CRITICAL READING SCORE: Unit 14

# GROUP THREE

*"The Cavalry" must have wondered what was going on. Reports of UFO sightings in northwest Sweden were multiplying, and the national defense agency was baffled. The most interesting report came from a man named Anders. While walking home one night, Anders claimed a cone of bright light covered him and then drew him upward into an object. Anders couldn't tell the Swedish authorities what happened next.*

# The Wave That Hit Sweden

Perhaps it was the full moon that gave Anders (not his real name) the idea to walk home from the party the night of March 23, 1974. The three-mile walk in the cool, fresh air might have seemed a welcome change from the stuffy, smoke-filled hall where the party had been held. On the other hand, in light of what happened that night, there are those who later argued that Anders did not act of his own accord. Instead, his actions were controlled by an outside force! Whatever the reason for Anders' decision to walk home, what he experienced would forever change his life.

Anders remembers leaving the party around midnight. To save time, he took a route through the woods toward his home in Lindholmen, Sweden, which is northwest of Stockholm. The moon glinting on the snowy ground made it easy to find his way. As he neared a bend in the road, he noticed a bright light ahead of him that seemed to be getting stronger. Fearing that a car was about to hit him, he leaped off the road and threw himself to the ground.

But Anders never felt the icy ground. Instead, he felt himself being drawn upward into a cone of light extending from some object overhead! Then his mind went blank. Anders' next memory was greeting his concerned wife at his own front door,

unable to explain the bleeding wound on his forehead and the burn on his cheek.

After Anders reported the incident to "The Cavalry," as the division of the Swedish national defense is known, it was not long before the local press caught on to the story. What had happened to Anders that night? Had he simply fallen asleep and had strange dreams? Or had he been abducted by a UFO? Convinced he had not been dreaming, Anders agreed with local UFO investigator Sten Lindgren to try hypnosis. Perhaps then he might recall some of the details of his strange experience.

What an experience it was! During two sessions with Dr. Ture Arvidsson, Anders revealed that after he was sucked into the light, he found himself confronted by four semitransparent beings. They wore hoods and appeared to be slightly glowing. Somehow the beings communicated through a series of musical tones. At some point the beings pierced Anders' forehead with a probelike instrument, causing his forehead to bleed.

About a year after the bizarre incident, Anders received a message in a dream: "You have had my sword within you for a year, but you don't know for what to use it." Apparently, Anders is still waiting to find out.

Although Anders was the only witness

to his encounter, his story was taken quite seriously. For several weeks there had been an amazing wave of UFO reports in the area. The Cavalry had even set up a "sky watch." Although nothing much was spotted, a witness did come forward to confirm the cone of light that Anders had seen, at exactly the same time and place. Unfortunately, her view had been obstructed by trees. It would have been impossible for her to see Anders from where she stood.

Within a two-hour period of Anders' abduction, authorities received more than 30 close encounter reports from the same area. But that was not the end of it. Less than 24 hours later, Mrs. H. Andersson and her family became another statistic in the incredible UFO wave.

Mrs. Andersson's first sighting took place at 7:25 in the evening of March 24. As she was driving with her children toward Vasaskolan, a school north of Lindholmen, she thought she saw a helicopter descend into a valley in proximity to the Anders abduction site. Unable to catch a further glimpse of the object, she continued on to her parents' home. During her visit there, the TV reception was poor, and the telephone was out of order. Then the object reappeared. Both Mrs. Andersson and her parents saw a large, bright UFO moving through the nearby forest toward a gravel pit. Other witnesses, a 90-year-old retired blacksmith and a local woman, confirmed the sighting.

Mrs. Andersson and her children then drove to her brother's house. Both she and her brother saw the object. Later in the evening she left his house to drive home. Her brother and his daughter followed in the car behind. On the way Mrs. Andersson's brother noticed an object pass over the road. He sped up to his sister and honked his horn to catch her attention. All of them watched in amazement as the object disappeared near a farm.

The UFO, however, was still not finished with Mrs. Andersson. Orange-colored objects high in the sky followed her car as she drove.

One of the objects swept a beam of light across the car before it and the others disappeared.

As the head of a local support group for UFO victims, Mrs. Andersson had heard her share of unpleasant stories. Her own was no exception. "It was so horrible I wish it had never happened," she said. "I got the impression that we were checked out by someone— like a big torch that swept the area."

Whatever the purpose of the "torch," it left its mark on Mrs. Andersson and her children. The children suffered headaches and stomachaches for some time afterward. Mrs. Andersson herself had severe pain in her kidneys for days. Still, the Anderssons

are thankful that their encounter went no further. Countless others throughout the world claim that they have not been so lucky. ■

*If you have been timed while reading this selection, enter your reading time below. Then turn to the Words-per-Minute table on page 155 and look up your reading speed (words per minute). Enter your reading speed on the graph on page 156.*

READING TIME: Unit 15

_____ : _____

*Minutes*      *Seconds*

# How well did you read?

- *Answer the four types of questions that follow. The directions for each type of question tell you how to mark your answers.*

- *When you have finished all four exercises, check your work by using the answer key on page 152. For each right answer, put a check mark ( ✓ ) on the line beside the box. For each wrong answer, write the correct answer on the line.*

- *For scoring each exercise, follow the directions below the questions.*

## A  FINDING THE MAIN IDEA

Look at the three statements below. One expresses the main idea of the story you just read. A good main idea statement answers two questions: it tells *who* or *what* is the subject of the story, and it answers the understood question *does what?* or *is what?* Another statement is *too broad;* it is vague and doesn't tell much about the topic of the story. The third statement is *too narrow;* it tells about only one part of the story.

Match the statements with the three answer choices below by writing the letter of each answer in the box in front of the statement it goes with.

**M—Main Idea**     **B—Too Broad**     **N—Too Narrow**

____  ☐ 1. Government officials in Sweden took the numerous reports of UFO encounters seriously.

____  ☐ 2. For several weeks in 1974, Anders, Andersson, and many others reported encounters in a region near Stockholm, Sweden.

____  ☐ 3. At first, Anders could not remember anything that happened after he left the party.

____ Score 15 points for a correct *M* answer
____ Score 5 points for each correct *B* or *N* answer
____ TOTAL SCORE: Finding the Main Idea

## B RECALLING FACTS

How well do you remember the facts in the story you just read? Put an *x* in the box in front of the correct answer to each of the multiple-choice questions below.

1. Anders was abducted
   - ____ ☐ a. while at a party.
   - ____ ☐ b. while walking home.
   - ____ ☐ c. outside his home.

2. The alien beings communicated with Anders
   - ____ ☐ a. through musical tones.
   - ____ ☐ b. by using mental imagery.
   - ____ ☐ c. with sign language.

3. Around the time of Anders' abduction
   - ____ ☐ a. many other abductions were reported.
   - ____ ☐ b. over 30 close encounters were reported.
   - ____ ☐ c. many homes lost electrical power.

4. After their UFO encounter, the Andersson children
   - ____ ☐ a. suffered no side effects.
   - ____ ☐ b. had nightmares.
   - ____ ☐ c. had headaches and stomachaches.

5. Mrs. Andersson
   - ____ ☐ a. heads a support group for UFO victims.
   - ____ ☐ b. works as a teacher.
   - ____ ☐ c. trains UFO researchers.

Score 5 points for each correct answer

____ TOTAL SCORE: Recalling Facts

## C MAKING INFERENCES

An inference is a judgment that is made or an idea that is arrived at based on facts or on information that is given. You make an inference when you understand something that is *not* stated directly but that is *implied,* or suggested, by the facts that are given.

Below are five statements that are judgments or ideas that have been arrived at from the facts of the story. Write the letter *C* in the box in front of each statement that is a correct inference. Write the letter *F* in front of each faulty inference.

**C—Correct Inference      F—Faulty Inference**

- ____ ☐ 1. Anders' decision to walk home may have been controlled by alien beings.
- ____ ☐ 2. If Anders had decided not to walk home, he may not have been abducted.
- ____ ☐ 3. Mrs. Andersson wasn't interested in Anders' UFO experience.
- ____ ☐ 4. UFOs were common in Sweden in the 1970s.
- ____ ☐ 5. Without hypnosis, Anders would probably not have remembered the details of his UFO encounter.

Score 5 points for each correct answer

____ TOTAL SCORE: Making Inferences

## D  USING WORDS PRECISELY

Each of the numbered sentences below contains an underlined word or phrase from the story you have just read. Under the sentence are three definitions. One is a *synonym*, a word that means the same or almost the same thing: *big* and *large*. One is an *antonym*, a word that has the opposite or nearly opposite meaning: *love* and *hate*. One is an unrelated word; it has a completely *different* meaning. Match the definitions with the three answer choices by writing the letter that stands for each answer in the box in front of the definition it goes with.

**S—Synonym    A—Antonym    D—Different**

1. . . . there are those who later argued that Anders did not act <u>of his own accord</u>.

____  ☐ a. voluntarily

____  ☐ b. unwillingly

____  ☐ c. politely

2. Anders found himself confronted by four <u>semitransparent</u> beings.

____  ☐ a. partially visible

____  ☐ b. wholesome

____  ☐ c. well-defined

3. For several weeks there had been an amazing <u>wave</u> of UFO reports in the area.

____  ☐ a. decrease

____  ☐ b. surge

____  ☐ c. column

4. Unfortunately, her view had been <u>obstructed</u> by trees.

____  ☐ a. hindered

____  ☐ b. blocked

____  ☐ c. free of obstacles

5. . . . she thought she saw a helicopter descend into a valley <u>in proximity</u> to the Anders' abduction site.

____  ☐ a. on the border of

____  ☐ b. far from

____  ☐ c. close to

____  Score 3 points for each correct *S* answer

____  Score 1 point for each correct *A* or *D* answer

____  TOTAL SCORE: Using Words Precisely

- *Enter the four total scores in the spaces below, and add them together to find your Critical Reading Score. Then record your Critical Reading Score on the graph on page 157.*

_____  Finding the Main Idea
_____  Recalling Facts
_____  Making Inferences
_____  Using Words Precisely

_____  CRITICAL READING SCORE:  Unit 15

Travis Walton's bizarre experience was the most publicized close encounter of the 1970s. After a day's work of cutting trees in an Arizona forest, Walton's crew watched in horror as Travis ran toward a golden UFO. The woodcutter later wrote a book called **The Walton Experience,** *in which he describes traveling on a spaceship and meeting five-foot-tall aliens with large hairless heads. Travis's boss, Michael Rogers, drew the illustrations for the book.*

# The Woodcutter's Tale

When the United States government offered Travis Walton the job of clearing trees in Arizona's Sitgraves National Park, the 22-year-old woodcutter jumped at the chance. The job would pay good money to the seven-man crew that included Travis and his brother Duane. However, if Travis had known what lay in store for him, he might never have agreed to set foot in the vast forest.

Around 5:00 in the evening on November 5, 1975, the men were driving home in their truck after finishing a day's work of tree-thinning when the driver suddenly slammed on the brakes. Near the road, hovering about 15 feet off the ground, was a large golden UFO! The men later described the object as saucer-shaped, with windows and a cupola on top. While his six co-workers stared dumbfounded, Travis jumped from the truck and, ignoring the cries of his friends, ran toward the glowing object. Suddenly a beam of blue light shot at him, lifting him in the air and throwing him to the ground. Thinking he had been killed, Travis's terrified friends raced away in their truck and headed to the police station in Heber.

Sheriff Ellison was sufficiently impressed by the young men's story to order an investigation. "One of the men was weeping," the sheriff recalled. "If they were lying, they were . . . good actors."

But when they arrived at the site where the woodcutters claimed the incident had occurred, the investigating team was in for a big surprise. Travis Walton was nowhere to be found!

While a search party combed the woods for the missing man, rumors abounded. Had Travis been murdered by his friends, who invented a story to cover up the deed? Was Travis Walton's disappearance part of an elaborate money-making plot? Or had Travis's body been carried off by the UFO?

Whatever the explanation, after five days of searching there was still no sign of Travis Walton. To help stifle rumors, on the morning of November 10 Travis's six co-workers agreed to take a lie detector test. The results were a disappointment to the many skeptics following the case. "I gotta say they passed," said Cy Gilson who administered the test to five of the men. The sixth man was reportedly too upset to take the test.

If those who believed in a murder plot needed any further proof of the wood-cutters' truthfulness, it arrived in a form that was hard to dispute. On the evening of November 10 Travis Walton reappeared! Obviously in a confused mental state, Travis insisted he had no memory of what had happened. However, with the help of an experienced hypnotist, the young man was eventually able to recall what was to become one of the most widely publicized cases in UFO history.

After being zapped by the blue beam, Travis claimed he was abducted by the UFO. When he gained consciousness, he found himself lying on a metal table surrounded by odd-looking creatures about five feet tall, with pale, hairless skin, and large domed heads. Although their eyes were huge, the rest of their features were reduced in size.

Travis panicked at the sight of the aliens. He struck out at one of them and was able to run into another room. There he met a more humanlike being wearing a blue uniform and a helmet. That being led Travis to a large building where several UFOs were parked. Three other humanlike beings, two men and a woman dressed in blue coveralls and helmets, led him to a table. When they placed a mask over his face, Travis lost consciousness. He remembered nothing until he awoke near a phone booth on a road outside Heber, a UFO rising above him.

Although Travis Walton's fantastic tale was far from the first UFO abduction story to become news, it seemed to inspire more than its share of debate. Skeptics and believers argued endlessly as to whether or not the young woodcutter was telling the truth. Adding fuel to the fire, UFO investigators uncovered information that supported both sides.

Travis Walton's detractors pointed out that the young man had once been in trouble with the law for forging checks. He also was known by his friends as a "UFO freak"; he had been fascinated by UFOs for years and had often said that he wanted to contact one. Travis told friends that if he was ever picked up by a UFO, he would try to convince the occupants to pick up his brother Duane as well so that they could share the experience.

Skeptics also noted that the Walton family did not seem upset during Travis's disappearance. Duane repeatedly stated that he was certain his brother had not been harmed and would be returned to the same location where he had disappeared.

Another factor that went against Travis was his failure of a lie detector test given by an experienced operator four days after his return. Although he passed another test given a few months later, skeptics discounted the results of the second test. They also questioned the test results of Travis's co-workers, claiming that the operator had not conducted the tests properly.

Despite the negative aspects of the case, Travis Walton has his supporters. Experienced investigators, including UFO researcher Dr. J. Allen Hynek, believed he was telling the truth. Many of those involved in the case claim that it was handled poorly by the news media. In fact, Travis had such a difficult time with the press that he kept an unlisted telephone number for nine years following his experience.

Continuing to maintain that he is telling the truth, Travis Walton has exacted his revenge on the press. He wrote a book about his abduction, one of the first on that subject to be accompanied by a public relations campaign. The fact that *The Walton Experience* may have been written by a ghostwriter does little to discourage those who believe that Travis *is* telling the truth as he saw it. And although Travis has even appeared on TV, not one of the six other witnesses of the encounter has ever tried to make money by denouncing his story. ■

*If you have been timed while reading this selection, enter your reading time below. Then turn to the Words-per-Minute table on page 155 and look up your reading speed (words per minute). Enter your reading speed on the graph on page 156.*

```
READING TIME: Unit 16

_____ : _____
Minutes        Seconds
```

# How well did you read?

- *Answer the four types of questions that follow. The directions for each type of question tell you how to mark your answers.*

- *When you have finished all four exercises, check your work by using the answer key on page 152. For each right answer, put a check mark (✓) on the line beside the box. For each wrong answer, write the correct answer on the line.*

- *For scoring each exercise, follow the directions below the questions.*

## A | FINDING THE MAIN IDEA

Look at the three statements below. One expresses the main idea of the story you just read. A good main idea statement answers two questions: it tells *who* or *what* is the subject of the story, and it answers the understood question *does what?* or *is what?* Another statement is *too broad;* it is vague and doesn't tell much about the topic of the story. The third statement is *too narrow;* it tells about only one part of the story.

Match the statements with the three answer choices below by writing the letter of each answer in the box in front of the statement it goes with.

**M—Main Idea      B—Too Broad      N—Too Narrow**

_____ ☐ 1. Travis Walton wrote about his UFO abduction in a book called *The Walton Experience.*

_____ ☐ 2. Travis Walton's UFO encounter in Arizona in 1975 remains the subject of much debate.

_____ ☐ 3. Travis Walton was involved in one of the most widely publicized cases in UFO history.

_____ Score 15 points for a correct *M* answer
_____ Score 5 points for each correct *B* or *N* answer
_____ TOTAL SCORE: Finding the Main Idea

## B RECALLING FACTS

How well do you remember the facts in the story you just read?
Put an x in the box in front of the correct answer to each of the
multiple-choice questions below.

1. The UFO Travis Walton saw was shaped like a
   - ____ ☐ a. ball.
   - ____ ☐ b. cupola.
   - ____ ☐ c. saucer.

2. Sheriff Ellison
   - ____ ☐ a. doubted the young men's story.
   - ____ ☐ b. was impressed enough by the story to order an investigation.
   - ____ ☐ c. went looking for Travis Walton himself.

3. Some people thought the missing Travis Walton
   - ____ ☐ a. had been murdered.
   - ____ ☐ b. eagerly joined the aliens on a trip into outer space.
   - ____ ☐ c. was playing a practical joke on his friends.

4. When Travis Walton finally reappeared, he
   - ____ ☐ a. refused to say where he had been.
   - ____ ☐ b. had no memory of what had happened.
   - ____ ☐ c. said he was in hiding while writing a book.

5. One reason some people doubted Travis Walton was that he
   - ____ ☐ a. never had expressed any interest in UFOs.
   - ____ ☐ b. did not get along well with people.
   - ____ ☐ c. previously had been in trouble with the law.

Score 5 points for each correct answer

____ TOTAL SCORE: Recalling Facts

## C MAKING INFERENCES

An inference is a judgment that is made or an idea that is arrived
at based on facts or on information that is given. You make an
inference when you understand something that is *not* stated
directly but that is *implied,* or suggested, by the facts that are given.

Below are five statements that are judgments or ideas that have
been arrived at from the facts of the story. Write the letter *C* in
the box in front of each statement that is a correct inference. Write
the letter *F* in front of each faulty inference.

**C—Correct Inference      F—Faulty Inference**

- ____ ☐ 1. Travis Walton's story is the most fantastic of all UFO tales.
- ____ ☐ 2. Sheriff Ellison was a fair-minded man.
- ____ ☐ 3. The creatures abducted Travis Walton because of his deep interest in UFOs.
- ____ ☐ 4. Travis and Duane were friends as well as brothers.
- ____ ☐ 5. Travis Walton is benefiting from his UFO experience.

Score 5 points for each correct answer

____ TOTAL SCORE: Making Inferences

## D  USING WORDS PRECISELY

Each of the numbered sentences below contains an underlined word or phrase from the story you have just read. Under the sentence are three definitions. One is a *synonym*, a word that means the same or almost the same thing: *big* and *large*. One is an *antonym*, a word that has the opposite or nearly opposite meaning: *love* and *hate*. One is an unrelated word; it has a completely *different* meaning. Match the definitions with the three answer choices by writing the letter that stands for each answer in the box in front of the definition it goes with.

**S—Synonym    A—Antonym    D—Different**

1. The men later described the object as saucer-shaped, with windows and a <u>cupola</u> on top.

____ ☐ a. small dome or tower

____ ☐ b. flat roof

____ ☐ c. atrium

2. While his six co-workers stared <u>dumbfounded</u>, Walton jumped from the truck. . . .

____ ☐ a. in fear

____ ☐ b. calmly

____ ☐ c. amazed

3. While a search party combed the woods for the missing man, rumors <u>abounded</u>.

____ ☐ a. were plentiful

____ ☐ b. overflowed

____ ☐ c. were in short supply

4. Continuing to maintain that he is telling the truth, Travis Walton has <u>exacted</u> his revenge on the press.

____ ☐ a. asked for

____ ☐ b. correctly argued

____ ☐ c. demanded

5. The fact that *The Walton Experience* may have been written by a <u>ghostwriter</u> . . .

____ ☐ a. someone who steals another's ideas

____ ☐ b. someone who writes for another

____ ☐ c. an experienced author

____ Score 3 points for each correct *S* answer
____ Score 1 point for each correct *A* or *D* answer

____ TOTAL SCORE: Using Words Precisely

● *Enter the four total scores in the spaces below, and add them together to find your Critical Reading Score. Then record your Critical Reading Score on the graph on page 157.*

_____ Finding the Main Idea
_____ Recalling Facts
_____ Making Inferences
_____ Using Words Precisely

_____ CRITICAL READING SCORE: Unit 16

Men in Black. Are they FBI or CIA agents? Or are they alien creatures on a special mission? Researchers are stumped. They have talked with many people who claim to have had MIB visits. Their descriptions of the eerie beings are usually the same—so is their fear of them. Albert K. Bender, a UFO investigator, had a visit from the MIB. He later drew this sketch of one of the creatures.

# The Mysterious Men in Black

Who are the Men in Black? No one is quite certain. Although people claim to have seen and talked with these eerie beings, there is no hard evidence that they even exist. Still, the creatures are a very curious—and frightening—part of the mystery that surrounds UFOs.

Since the late 1950s the ominous Men in Black (MIB) have called on UFO witnesses or researchers. Most wear somber attire—neat black suits, black ties, and white shirts; sometimes they dress in military uniforms. They drive shiny black cars, often Cadillacs. They may appear alone, but most often they travel in threes. While their height varies, they are usually dark-skinned and have slanted eyes. They show little emotion and are almost robotlike.

The reason for their visits is very clear: to frighten people into keeping quiet about their UFO experiences. Some MIB instill fear by their presence alone. Others have allegedly threatened their victims, but no one has ever reported being physically hurt by the unwelcome visitors. Still, MIB incidents are so unsettling that many victims feel extremely upset, even ill, for days afterward.

Rex Heflin, a former California highway inspector, had a MIB visit in 1967, two years after he encountered a UFO. Heflin's story, along with several photographs he had taken of the UFO with a Polaroid camera, appeared in magazines and newspapers across the country. After the story was published, a man claiming to be from the air force convinced Heflin to give him the original prints. Later, however, the air force denied that it had sent anyone to talk with Heflin. The original prints were never found.

Two years after the puzzling visit, a team investigating UFOs wanted to learn more about Heflin's story. After talking with the researchers, Heflin got another strange visit. A man wearing an air force uniform knocked on his door. He gave his name as Captain C. H. Edmonds. "Are you going to try to get your originals back?" he asked. When Heflin replied "no," Captain Edmonds looked very relieved. Then he struck up an odd conversation about subjects like the Bermuda Triangle, a section of the Atlantic Ocean where ships and planes have mysteriously disappeared.

While they were talking, Heflin noticed a large dark car parked across the street. There were letters on the door that he could not make out. He could see a man in the back seat who seemed to be fiddling with some sort of machine that gave off a strange violet glow. Heflin assumed that he was being photographed and recorded.

For some time after the incident Heflin believed his phone was tapped. His mail was opened. And neighbors told him that men in uniform came to his door several times while he was away. Who were these men, and who was Captain Edmonds? When investigators tried to locate the captain, they reached a dead end. There was no such person in the air force.

In 1973 Stan Gordon, the head of a UFO group in Pennsylvania, investigated a call from a woman who said she had seen a space creature with big feet outside her home. After talking with the woman, Gordon and two others were taking pictures of the footprints when a man in a black suit drove up in a station wagon. He jumped out of the car and started asking a lot of questions. "The woman who lives here says she saw a creature from outer space," Gordon explained to the man. "We're just taking some pictures." That was all the stranger needed to hear. He grabbed the camera and tore out the film. Then he destroyed the footprints and drove away.

Dr. J. Allen Hynek, a well-known UFO investigator, made a special trip to Mexico in 1974. He planned to talk to a young Mexican pilot named Carlos Monteil who had reported seeing three UFOs during a flight to Mexico City. After talking for two hours, they agreed to meet again the next morning. The pilot, however, never showed up. According to a friend of Monteil's, the pilot had been visited by the Men in Black. It had happened while he was driving home from his interview with Dr. Hynek. The friend said Monteil's car had been followed and forced off the road. Two men jumped out of their car and warned Monteil that he had better keep quiet about UFOs—for his own good. Afraid for his life, Monteil decided that he had said enough.

Dr. Herbert Hopkins also had a MIB visit. While home alone one night in 1976, he received a telephone call from a man who said he was part of a New Jersey team researching UFOs. He wanted to discuss one of the doctor's cases—a patient who claimed to have been kidnapped by a UFO. Seconds after the call ended a visitor dressed in a black suit, black tie, and gleaming white shirt arrived at Hopkins's door. The man was totally bald, had deathly white skin, and appeared to be wearing lipstick. "He looks like an undertaker," Hopkins thought. Nevertheless, he invited the stranger in.

After a long conversation Hopkins noticed the man's speech was slowing, and his movements were unsteady. "My energy is running low now," said the man, and he bid the doctor goodbye. The incident left Hopkins badly shaken. He wondered why he had been so willing to talk with a stranger. To his relief, he never heard from the "researcher" again.

Another MIB case involved a family that wishes to remain anonymous. Several weeks after seeing a UFO the family received an unexpected visitor. Unaccustomed to strangers in their area, they were startled to find a seven-foot-tall man with ashen skin standing on their front porch. He had an extremely small head and very thin arms and legs. Although it was bitterly cold, the man was dressed in only a light jacket and a fur hat. He wore some sort of badge, which he quickly removed. He explained that he worked for an insurance company and flashed a card that disappeared before anyone could read it. The stranger said his purpose was to inform the family about an inheritance. There was a lot of money involved, but he would not give any details.

When the man sat down, the oldest daughter in the family noticed something very weird: the man's pant leg had pulled up slightly, revealing a green wire that ran out of his sock and directly into his leg! When the eccentric visitor rose to leave, a large black car with two passengers suddenly pulled up to the curb outside the family's home. The visitor hurried to the car, which drove off into the night with its headlights turned off.

Although researchers have investigated scores of visits by the Men in Black, not one trace of evidence proves that they exist. Still, the stories—and the questions—persist. Could the Men in Black be government agents, perhaps working for the FBI or CIA? Or could they be extraterrestrials impersonating human beings? Witnesses agree that the "men" do not look human and often seem puzzled by such mundane items as ballpoint pens or eating utensils. Is their clothing and makeup an attempt to blend in, to look "normal"? If so, they are obviously confused. Does all this "prove" that they are from outer space? ■

*If you have been timed while reading this selection, enter your reading time below. Then turn to the Words-per-Minute table on page 155 and look up your reading speed (words per minute). Enter your reading speed on the graph on page 156.*

READING TIME: Unit 17

_____ : _____
*Minutes*        *Seconds*

# How well did you read?

- *Answer the four types of questions that follow. The directions for each type of question tell you how to mark your answers.*

- *When you have finished all four exercises, check your work by using the answer key on page 152. For each right answer, put a check mark (✓) on the line beside the box. For each wrong answer, write the correct answer on the line.*

- *For scoring each exercise, follow the directions below the questions.*

## A · FINDING THE MAIN IDEA

Look at the three statements below. One expresses the main idea of the story you just read. A good main idea statement answers two questions: it tells *who* or *what* is the subject of the story, and it answers the understood question *does what?* or *is what?* Another statement is *too broad;* it is vague and doesn't tell much about the topic of the story. The third statement is *too narrow;* it tells about only one part of the story.

Match the statements with the three answer choices below by writing the letter of each answer in the box in front of the statement it goes with.

**M—Main Idea**      **B—Too Broad**      **N—Too Narrow**

_____ ☐ 1. Many UFO witnesses claim they have been visited by mysterious Men in Black who try to frighten them into silence.

_____ ☐ 2. Starting in the late 1950s, people began reporting unexpected and disturbing visits by mysterious Men in Black.

_____ ☐ 3. The Men in Black are eerie, robotlike creatures with dark or very pale skin and slanted eyes.

_____ Score 15 points for a correct *M* answer
_____ Score 5 points for each correct *B* or *N* answer
_____ TOTAL SCORE: Finding the Main Idea

## B RECALLING FACTS

How well do you remember the facts in the story you just read?
Put an x in the box in front of the correct answer to each of the
multiple-choice questions below.

1. People who claim to have met the Men in Black say they
   ___ ☐ a. are usually kind and gentle.
   ___ ☐ b. seldom threaten people.
   ___ ☐ c. never hurt anyone.

2. The MIB visited Rex Heflin because they wanted to
   ___ ☐ a. kill him.
   ___ ☐ b. take his UFO photographs.
   ___ ☐ c. abduct him.

3. The Men in Black
   ___ ☐ a. work for the FBI.
   ___ ☐ b. have never been identified.
   ___ ☐ c. are really UFO investigators.

4. Carlos Monteil was a
   ___ ☐ a. young pilot.
   ___ ☐ b. UFO researcher.
   ___ ☐ c. former highway inspector.

5. All the witnesses agree that the
   ___ ☐ a. Men in Black do not seem human.
   ___ ☐ b. air force is behind the visits.
   ___ ☐ c. visits may have been dreams.

Score 5 points for each correct answer

___ TOTAL SCORE: Recalling Facts

## C MAKING INFERENCES

An inference is a judgment that is made or an idea that is arrived
at based on facts or on information that is given. You make an
inference when you understand something that is *not* stated
directly but that is *implied,* or suggested, by the facts that are given.

Below are five statements that are judgments or ideas that have
been arrived at from the facts of the story. Write the letter *C* in
the box in front of each statement that is a correct inference. Write
the letter *F* in front of each faulty inference.

**C—Correct Inference     F—Faulty Inference**

___ ☐ 1. The Men in Black conceal their true identities.

___ ☐ 2. Most of the people visited by the Men in Black
         had overactive imaginations.

___ ☐ 3. The mission of the Men in Black is a mystery.

___ ☐ 4. Rex Heflin was an observant person.

___ ☐ 5. There is no evidence that the Men in Black work
         for the FBI or the CIA.

Score 5 points for each correct answer

___ TOTAL SCORE: Making Inferences

## D USING WORDS PRECISELY

Each of the numbered sentences below contains an underlined word or phrase from the story you have just read. Under the sentence are three definitions. One is a *synonym,* a word that means the same or almost the same thing: *big* and *large*. One is an *antonym,* a word that has the opposite or nearly opposite meaning: *love* and *hate*. One is an unrelated word; it has a completely *different* meaning. Match the definitions with the three answer choices by writing the letter that stands for each answer in the box in front of the definition it goes with.

**S—Synonym     A—Antonym     D—Different**

1. Most wear <u>somber</u> attire—neat black suits, black ties, and white shirts. . . .

   —— ☐ a. heavy

   —— ☐ b. dazzling

   —— ☐ c. dismal

2. Some MIB <u>instill</u> fear by their presence alone.

   —— ☐ a. prevent or eliminate

   —— ☐ b. cause or produce

   —— ☐ c. frighten or scare

3. . . . they were startled to find a seven-foot-tall man with <u>ashen</u> skin standing on their front porch.

   —— ☐ a. pale

   —— ☐ b. dirty

   —— ☐ c. tanned

4. . . . the <u>eccentric</u> visitor rose to leave. . . .

   —— ☐ a. ordinary

   —— ☐ b. unpredictable

   —— ☐ c. peculiar

5. Witnesses agree that the "men" do not look human and often seem puzzled by . . . <u>mundane</u> items. . . .

   —— ☐ a. earthly

   —— ☐ b. common

   —— ☐ c. unfamiliar

—— Score 3 points for each correct *S* answer
—— Score 1 point for each correct *A* or *D* answer
—— TOTAL SCORE: Using Words Precisely

- *Enter the four total scores in the spaces below, and add them together to find your Critical Reading Score. Then record your Critical Reading Score on the graph on page 157.*

————————————————————————
———— Finding the Main Idea
———— Recalling Facts
———— Making Inferences
———— Using Words Precisely
———— CRITICAL READING SCORE: Unit 17
————————————————————————

'Twas the night after Christmas, and all through the house, nothing was stirring not even . . . Whitley Strieber woke up just as the creature opened his bedroom door. As the small figure, dressed in what looked like armor, rushed toward him, Strieber fainted. The next morning Strieber remembered nothing about his strange encounter. Weeks later the whole story began to unfold.

# The Chosen One

Starting in the fall of 1985, author Whitley Strieber had developed an unusual habit. Whenever he and his wife and son stayed at their remote cabin in upstate New York, Strieber would make a secret tour of the house before going to bed. First he would turn on the burglar alarm. Then he would look everywhere for hidden intruders. It was not until he had peered into every closet and looked under every bed that he could finally relax.

On the night of December 26, 1985, Strieber had completed his rounds and fallen peacefully asleep. But at some point he was awakened by a strange "whooshing, swirling noise" coming from the living room downstairs. It sounded, he said, "as if a large number of people were moving rapidly around the room."

Frightened and curious, he checked the burglar alarm panel beside the bed. It was still armed, showing that no door or window had been opened. Relieved, Strieber settled back into bed when he noticed that one of the doors leading into the bedroom was opening! Strieber's heart started racing as a small being edged around the door. The being wore a smooth, rounded hat with a sharp rim that jutted out about four inches. As the being moved closer, Strieber could make out two dark holes for eyes and the black line of a mouth. A square plate resembling an armored vest covered the creature from chin to waist, and a similar plate extended from the lower waist to just above the knees.

Suddenly the creature rushed into the room and Strieber fainted. The next thing he remembered was being moved out of the room, his body paralyzed. He passed out again.

When he awoke he was sitting in a small depression in the woods, unable to move any part of his body except for his eyes. A small being wearing a bodysuit was sitting on the ground nearby, its slender arms clasped around its knees. The face had two dark eyeholes and a mouth that was no more than a round hole. For some reason he could not explain, Strieber thought of the being as female.

Strieber said next he was swept into the air until he was floating above the treetops. Then a gray floor obscured his vision, and he was sitting in a messy round room. The room was dirty and confining, the air very dry. Strieber was seated on a bench while tiny beings darted this way and that around him. At one point he was shown a small gray box that contained a shiny needle, so thin it was almost invisible. He became aware that the beings planned to insert the needle in his brain! Strieber started screaming, overcome with terror. Then he heard a bang! and a crash! Despite his protests, the operation with the needle had taken place. Defeated, Strieber sank down into "a cradle of tiny arms."

Sometime later one of the creatures made an incision on Strieber's right forefinger, which surprisingly caused no pain. "Why are you doing this?" he asked. "You are our chosen one," a voice answered.

Although the creatures' hands were soft and soothing, Strieber felt very distressed whenever he was touched, as if he were being handled by insects. In addition to the small, robotlike being that had entered his bedroom, he became aware of three other kinds of creatures. The largest group consisted of short, stocky figures wearing dark blue coveralls. These figures had wide faces with dark, glittering, deep-set eyes, flat noses, and broad, almost humanlike mouths. Two other types of creatures did not look at all human. The femalelike creature was one of these: about five feet tall, very slender and delicate, with huge black slanted eyes and a tiny nose and mouth. The last type was somewhat smaller, with round black eyes.

Strieber could not remember returning to his own room. And when he awoke the next morning, he did not recall what had taken place during the night. His wife, unaware that anything unusual had happened, had slept soundly. During the day Strieber felt exhausted and uneasy without knowing why. He went to bed complaining of chills and a fever and with strange recollections swirling through his head.

The next few weeks were a time of turmoil for Strieber and his family. A professional writer, he could not concentrate on his work. He had wild, unpredictable mood swings and easily became confused. A sudden infection on his right forefinger grew worse despite treatment. From time to time mental pictures would flood into his head, leaving him sweating and gasping, his heart pounding.

In an effort to ignore his symptoms, Strieber began reading a book about UFOs that he had received as a Christmas present. But after a few pages he became so terrified that he slammed the book shut. Could he have been kidnapped by visitors from outer space? Unwilling to face what he knew to be the truth, Strieber vowed to keep the whole horrifying ordeal a secret.

But a few days later, fearful that he either had a brain tumor or was losing his mind, Strieber sought professional help. He called Budd Hopkins, a well-known UFO researcher whom he had read about.

Strieber learned from Hopkins that he was not alone! There were many other people who had had encounters much like his own. Strieber decided on a course of action. He was sure that hypnosis would help him deal with his experience.

In a series of sessions with Dr. Donald Klein, a therapist in New York City, Strieber got more than he bargained for. His experience in December 1985 had not been his first! Through hypnosis Strieber learned about many other encounters that had occurred since the age of 12. It also seemed that his son may have had at least one encounter as well.

Whitley Strieber wrote about his experiences in a best-selling book, *Communion*, published in 1988. His critics are convinced that what he wrote is fiction. But his supporters—and there are many—are convinced of his sincerity. Strieber defends his story in these words: "It is a true story, as true as I know how to describe it."

It is true that the author has become very wealthy as a result of his experiences. *Communion* was made into a popular movie, for which Strieber wrote the screenplay, and a second book was also a best seller. But he staunchly denies they are works of fiction. Two lie detector tests he has taken suggest that he is telling the truth.

"When you read this incredible story, do not be too skeptical," the author advises. Strieber remembers that he too was once an "indifferent skeptic" about UFOs and extraterrestrials. Now, all that has changed for him. Convinced that UFOs and extra-terrestrials are real, he asks new questions: What more will we learn about worlds beyond our own? Will we have the courage to face whatever awaits us there? ■

*If you have been timed while reading this selection, enter your reading time below. Then turn to the Words-per-Minute table on page 155 and look up your reading speed (words per minute). Enter your reading speed on the graph on page 156.*

READING TIME: Unit 18

_____ : _____
*Minutes*      *Seconds*

# How well did you read?

- *Answer the four types of questions that follow. The directions for each type of question tell you how to mark your answers.*

- *When you have finished all four exercises, check your work by using the answer key on page 152. For each right answer, put a check mark (✓) on the line beside the box. For each wrong answer, write the correct answer on the line.*

- *For scoring each exercise, follow the directions below the questions.*

## A · FINDING THE MAIN IDEA

Look at the three statements below. One expresses the main idea of the story you just read. A good main idea statement answers two questions: it tells *who* or *what* is the subject of the story, and it answers the understood question *does what?* or *is what?* Another statement is *too broad;* it is vague and doesn't tell much about the topic of the story. The third statement is *too narrow;* it tells about only one part of the story.

Match the statements with the three answer choices below by writing the letter of each answer in the box in front of the statement it goes with.

**M—Main Idea    B—Too Broad    N—Too Narrow**

_____ ☐ 1. Some UFO witnesses become rich and famous as a result of their encounters with alien creatures.

_____ ☐ 2. Whitley Strieber wrote a best-selling book called *Communion* about his experiences.

_____ ☐ 3. Through hypnosis, Whitley Strieber discovered that he had alien encounters beginning in his early teens.

_____ Score 15 points for a correct *M* answer

_____ Score 5 points for each correct *B* or *N* answer

**_____ TOTAL SCORE:** Finding the Main Idea

## B   RECALLING FACTS

How well do you remember the facts in the story you just read? Put an *x* in the box in front of the correct answer to each of the multiple-choice questions below.

1. The encounter described in the story took place in
   - ___ ☐ a. upstate New York.
   - ___ ☐ b. New York City.
   - ___ ☐ c. Whitley Strieber's imagination.

2. When the creature rushed into Strieber's room, Strieber
   - ___ ☐ a. fainted.
   - ___ ☐ b. took a picture of the being.
   - ___ ☐ c. screamed in fear.

3. The creature that entered Strieber's room
   - ___ ☐ a. looked like a human.
   - ___ ☐ b. wore dark blue coveralls.
   - ___ ☐ c. was a small robotlike being.

4. Immediately after the encounter, Strieber
   - ___ ☐ a. wrote a best-selling book.
   - ___ ☐ b. found his life in turmoil.
   - ___ ☐ c. woke his wife to tell her what had happened.

5. To learn more about what had happened to him, Strieber
   - ___ ☐ a. agreed to accompany the aliens to their planet.
   - ___ ☐ b. underwent hypnosis.
   - ___ ☐ c. talked at length with the police.

Score 5 points for each correct answer

___ TOTAL SCORE:  Recalling Facts

## C   MAKING INFERENCES

An inference is a judgment that is made or an idea that is arrived at based on facts or on information that is given. You make an inference when you understand something that is *not* stated directly but that is *implied,* or suggested, by the facts that are given.

Below are five statements that are judgments or ideas that have been arrived at from the facts of the story. Write the letter *C* in the box in front of each statement that is a correct inference. Write the letter *F* in front of each faulty inference.

**C—Correct Inference      F—Faulty Inference**

- ___ ☐ 1. The creature that invaded Whitley Strieber's room was not at all frightening.
- ___ ☐ 2. After the alien encounter, Strieber was worried about his health.
- ___ ☐ 3. Strieber was greatly influenced by his encounter.
- ___ ☐ 4. Strieber's book, *Communion,* is controversial.
- ___ ☐ 5. Hypnosis can be helpful in unlocking UFO mysteries from the minds of witnesses.

Score 5 points for each correct answer

___ TOTAL SCORE:  Making Inferences

## D USING WORDS PRECISELY

Each of the numbered sentences below contains an underlined word or phrase from the story you have just read. Under the sentence are three definitions. One is a *synonym,* a word that means the same or almost the same thing: *big* and *large.* One is an *antonym,* a word that has the opposite or nearly opposite meaning: *love* and *hate.* One is an unrelated word; it has a completely *different* meaning. Match the definitions with the three answer choices by writing the letter that stands for each answer in the box in front of the definition it goes with.

**S—Synonym     A—Antonym     D—Different**

1. The being wore a smooth, rounded hat with a sharp rim that jutted out about four inches.

____  ☐ a. unbent

____  ☐ b. shrank

____  ☐ c. extended

2. When he awoke he was sitting in a small depression in the woods. . . .

____  ☐ a. hole or dent

____  ☐ b. mound or pile

____  ☐ c. blank space

3. The next few weeks were a time of turmoil for Strieber and his family.

____  ☐ a. calmness

____  ☐ b. violence

____  ☐ c. confusion

4. *Communion* was made into a popular movie, for which Strieber wrote the screenplay. . . .

____  ☐ a. movie script

____  ☐ b. directions

____  ☐ c. theater script

5. But he staunchly denies they are works of fiction.

____  ☐ a. completely

____  ☐ b. firmly

____  ☐ c. weakly

____  Score 3 points for each correct *S* answer

____  Score 1 point for each correct *A* or *D* answer

____  TOTAL SCORE: Using Words Precisely

● *Enter the four total scores in the spaces below, and add them together to find your Critical Reading Score. Then record your Critical Reading Score on the graph on page 157.*

_____  Finding the Main Idea
_____  Recalling Facts
_____  Making Inferences
_____  Using Words Precisely

_____  CRITICAL READING SCORE: Unit 18

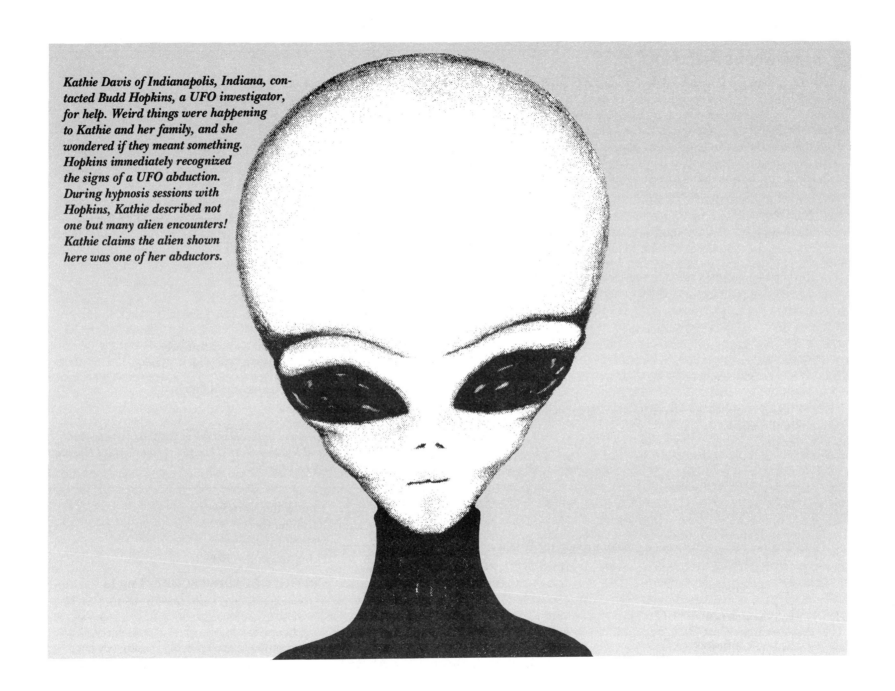

Kathie Davis of Indianapolis, Indiana, contacted Budd Hopkins, a UFO investigator, for help. Weird things were happening to Kathie and her family, and she wondered if they meant something. Hopkins immediately recognized the signs of a UFO abduction. During hypnosis sessions with Hopkins, Kathie described not one but many alien encounters! Kathie claims the alien shown here was one of her abductors.

# The Human Experiment

The Davis family (not their real name) was baffled. Clearly, something out of the ordinary had occurred in the backyard of their comfortable home in suburban Indianapolis, Indiana. In the middle of their lush lawn was a circle, eight feet in diameter, of brown, crumbling grass. Extending out from this circle in a straight line was a 3-foot-wide, 49-foot-long track that ended in a nearly perfect arc. Here, too, the grass looked scorched and withered as if it had been burned. The weird pattern appeared suddenly in July 1983, and months later new grass still refused to grow there.

What could have caused the strange marks? Robert Davis and his wife, Mary, had no idea. It was their grown daughter, Kathie, who began to piece things together. She remembered some odd events that had occurred about the time the pattern appeared on the lawn. A little before 9:00 P.M. on June 30, 1983, Kathie had noticed a "funny-colored" light from the pump house near the backyard swimming pool. Despite the eerie feeling the light gave her, Kathie took her mother Mary's advice "not to worry about it." But when Kathie left for her friend Dee Anne's house a few minutes later, the pump house was dark. And the garage door, which had been shut, was now inexplicably open.

Shortly after reaching Dee Anne's house,

Kathie received an unsettling phone call from her usually calm mother. Mary Davis told her daughter she had noticed a round ball of light surrounding the bird feeder in the backyard. "It was a pale white light . . . round and about as big as a basketball," she later described it. Although the light suddenly faded out, Mary felt uneasy enough to ask her daughter to return to investigate the strange goings-on.

Kathie arrived home around 9:30, took out her father's empty rifle for courage, and set out for the backyard. She didn't find any prowlers or see anything unusual, except that her normally rambunctious dog was cowering under her car. Kathie returned inside, after what she and her mother recalled was a period of no more than 10 minutes. Then Kathie went back to Dee Anne's, arriving a little after 11:00 P.M., and invited Dee Anne and her daughter, Tammy, to her house for a late-night swim. They returned to the Davises' around 11:30.

As Tammy walked barefoot toward the pool, she "stepped on a place where there wasn't any grass, and it felt warm, like warm cement." Tammy began to feel nauseated and dizzy. Then Dee Anne mentioned to Kathie that she felt uneasy, "like somebody's watching us." Kathie tried to reassure her friends, and soon after they all went into the pool. Minutes later they suddenly felt very

cold, despite the warm night. And Kathie started having trouble with her eyes. The three of them decided to get out of the pool. While Kathie was drying off, her vision grew hazy, and her eyes began to burn. She didn't think it was a reaction to the chlorine because she hadn't put her head under water. Kathie recalled seeing that "everything was white with halos around the lights." Kathie, Dee Anne, and Tammy left the backyard feeling "really sick."

Kathie was unwell for days afterward. Besides her eye problems, she suffered from nausea and began to lose her hair. She also felt a slight pain in her right ear and had trouble hearing for several weeks.

Shortly after these peculiar events, Kathie read a book called *Missing Time*. Written by Budd Hopkins, the book documented seven UFO abductions investigated by the author. Kathie was amazed to read details of experiences much like her own. She realized that she too had "missed time." On the night of June 30, she had somehow lost the hour between 10:00 and 11:00. Could she have been abducted by a UFO?

When Kathie decided to write to Hopkins about the backyard incident, she began to remember other curious events. Her sister Laura had once seen a silvery object with flashing lights hovering soundlessly over her car. Both Kathie and her mother had

had vivid "dreams" remarkably similar in content. Both women also have identical scars on their right legs.

When Budd Hopkins read Kathie's letter, he recognized at once the pattern of a UFO encounter. What he could not know was that he was about to become involved in what has been called the most significant case in UFO history.

Through the course of hundreds of interviews, phone calls, and letters, Hopkins gradually put together Kathie's incredible story. Kathie was able to recall under hypnosis what happened the night of June 30. The eerie lights in her backyard proved to be a landed, egg-shaped UFO. White globes of light surrounded her as she experienced the shock and pain of a blast of radiation, like a bolt of lightning. Kathie saw six bullet-shaped aliens, which she described as about her height, but with no distinct features. While she did not remember being inside the craft, Kathie did recall a "presence" gently holding her arm and inserting a pencil-like object in her ear.

By itself, Kathie's backyard encounter was no more remarkable than others Hopkins had studied. But as he continued his research with Kathie Davis, Hopkins made a startling discovery. Kathie had had many alien encounters throughout her life. And there would be more to come!

When she was very young, Kathie dreamed that her mother hid her in a closet to protect her from a threat in the sky. Oddly, her mother had a similar "dream." Another early event involved going to a strange house and meeting a "little boy." Hopkins believes this is a false memory implanted by an alien to disguise Kathie's abduction. It was during this abduction that a sample of Kathie's skin was taken, leaving the scar exactly like her mother's.

In December 1977 Kathie was abducted from a car in which she and two friends were riding. Her friends were paralyzed, unaware that Kathie was taken aboard a UFO. Several other abductions followed, including one in 1979 when a probe was inserted into Kathie's nose, possibly as a monitoring device.

Some months after contacting Budd Hopkins, Kathie was abducted again. Following a painful examination aboard a UFO, she awoke in her backyard, dressed in a nightgown. A further abduction took place in November 1983, during which Kathie was again subjected to a medical exam. Around this time Kathie accidentally saw an alien coming from her son Tommy's bedroom. It seems not only Kathie but also her two young sons had been abducted!

Why has Kathie Davis—and her family—been singled out for this unwanted attention? Hopkins is continuing to investigate the incidents as they unfold. For Kathie, the revelations—recalled mostly through hypnosis—are painful and disturbing.

"It's very difficult for me to accept this," Kathie admits. "There's a part of me that really does . . . and has known this for maybe nine years. But this is so farfetched and outrageous that I find it extremely difficult to really accept."

Although not all the evidence in the Kathie Davis case had been made public, what has been revealed is difficult for anyone to accept. Yet Kathie's story has been corroborated by family, friends, neighbors, and specialists. If Kathie Davis is telling the truth—and the evidence suggests that she is—then the repeated abductions of Kathie and her family imply that there is a disturbing purpose behind them. That purpose is almost unthinkable. Aliens are studying human beings as part of an ongoing experiment that is beyond our control. ∎

*If you have been timed while reading this selection, enter your reading time below. Then turn to the Words-per-Minute table on page 155 and look up your reading speed (words per minute). Enter your reading speed on the graph on page 156.*

READING TIME: Unit 19

_____ : _____
*Minutes*     *Seconds*

# How well did you read?

- *Answer the four types of questions that follow. The directions for each type of question tell you how to mark your answers.*

- *When you have finished all four exercises, check your work by using the answer key on page 152. For each right answer, put a check mark (✓) on the line beside the box. For each wrong answer, write the correct answer on the line.*

- *For scoring each exercise, follow the directions below the questions.*

## A  FINDING THE MAIN IDEA

Look at the three statements below. One expresses the main idea of the story you just read. A good main idea statement answers two questions: it tells *who* or *what* is the subject of the story, and it answers the understood question *does what?* or *is what?* Another statement is *too broad;* it is vague and doesn't tell much about the topic of the story. The third statement is *too narrow;* it tells about only one part of the story.

Match the statements with the three answer choices below by writing the letter of each answer in the box in front of the statement it goes with.

**M—Main Idea**     **B—Too Broad**     **N—Too Narrow**

_____ ☐ 1. The abductions of Kathie Davis and her family suggest they are part of a human experiment by aliens.

_____ ☐ 2. Like many other UFO victims, Kathie Davis experienced "missing time."

_____ ☐ 3. The Kathie Davis case has been called the most significant case in UFO history.

_____ Score 15 points for a correct *M* answer

_____ Score 5 points for each correct *B* or *N* answer

_____ TOTAL SCORE:  Finding the Main Idea

## B  RECALLING FACTS

How well do you remember the facts in the story you just read? Put an *x* in the box in front of the correct answer to each of the multiple-choice questions below.

1. The Davises live
   - ____ ☐ a. somewhere on the East Coast.
   - ____ ☐ b. in Indianapolis, Indiana.
   - ____ ☐ c. near a nuclear power plant.

2. Evidence of a UFO landing in the Davises' backyard was
   - ____ ☐ a. a withered tree.
   - ____ ☐ b. a large burned circle in the lawn.
   - ____ ☐ c. difficult to find.

3. Kathie Davis was abducted
   - ____ ☐ a. twice.
   - ____ ☐ b. three times.
   - ____ ☐ c. many times.

4. Kathie and her mother
   - ____ ☐ a. have identical scars on their right legs.
   - ____ ☐ b. look very much alike.
   - ____ ☐ c. are both psychic.

5. Kathie contacted Budd Hopkins
   - ____ ☐ a. after reading his book.
   - ____ ☐ b. because he was a good friend.
   - ____ ☐ c. after she was hypnotized.

Score 5 points for each correct answer

____ TOTAL SCORE: Recalling Facts

## C  MAKING INFERENCES

An inference is a judgment that is made or an idea that is arrived at based on facts or on information that is given. You make an inference when you understand something that is *not* stated directly but that is *implied,* or suggested, by the facts that are given.

Below are five statements that are judgments or ideas that have been arrived at from the facts of the story. Write the letter *C* in the box in front of each statement that is a correct inference. Write the letter *F* in front of each faulty inference.

**C—Correct Inference     F—Faulty Inference**

- ____ ☐ 1. Large doses of radiation can seriously affect humans.
- ____ ☐ 2. Budd Hopkins knows why the aliens have chosen the Davises for their experiments.
- ____ ☐ 3. Kathie Davis is eager to be abducted again.
- ____ ☐ 4. Aliens can control the memories of human beings.
- ____ ☐ 5. Kathie's mother was probably abducted by a UFO.

Score 5 points for each correct answer

____ TOTAL SCORE: Making Inferences

## D USING WORDS PRECISELY

Each of the numbered sentences below contains an underlined word or phrase from the story you have just read. Under the sentence are three definitions. One is a *synonym*, a word that means the same or almost the same thing: *big* and *large*. One is an *antonym*, a word that has the opposite or nearly opposite meaning: *love* and *hate*. One is an unrelated word; it has a completely *different* meaning. Match the definitions with the three answer choices by writing the letter that stands for each answer in the box in front of the definition it goes with.

**S—Synonym     A—Antonym     D—Different**

1. And the garage door, which had been shut, was now <u>inexplicably</u> open.

____ ☐ a. mysteriously

____ ☐ b. clearly

____ ☐ c. innocently

2. Kathie's dog was usually <u>rambunctious</u>.

____ ☐ a. controlled

____ ☐ b. deceptive

____ ☐ c. unruly

3. Kathie found her dog <u>cowering</u> under the car.

____ ☐ a. crawling

____ ☐ b. cringing

____ ☐ c. fearless

4. For Kathie, the <u>revelations</u> [of her experiences] are painful and disturbing.

____ ☐ a. secret or hidden

____ ☐ b. things made known

____ ☐ c. reactions

5. Yet Kathie's story has been <u>corroborated</u> by family, friends, neighbors, and specialists.

____ ☐ a. confirmed

____ ☐ b. imitated

____ ☐ c. denied

____ Score 3 points for each correct *S* answer
____ Score 1 point for each correct *A* or *D* answer

____ TOTAL SCORE: Using Words Precisely

● *Enter the four total scores in the spaces below, and add them together to find your Critical Reading Score. Then record your Critical Reading Score on the graph on page 157.*

_____ Finding the Main Idea
_____ Recalling Facts
_____ Making Inferences
_____ Using Words Precisely

_____ CRITICAL READING SCORE: Unit 19

*An "intellectual" arrived at Dan's house one day to talk about Dan's life on Earth. Dan claims he is an alien who "retired" to planet Earth, replacing a small boy who lived in the state of Washington. Now in his 40s, Dan dreams about returning to space. Is his life on Earth in limbo?*

# At Home in Space

UFOs and extraterrestrials have fascinated Dan since he was a youngster. Now a licensed airplane pilot in his mid-40s, Dan frequently watches the skies for UFOs, hoping to see one. He never thought he had a UFO encounter . . .

\* \* \*

"I try to remain open and objective," Dan began. "But it's odd. I've always had the feeling that I'm not native to here. Every time I look at the night sky, I have a nostalgic feeling, really at gut-level, that I want to go home."

Dr. Edith Fiore's eyes widened as she heard Dan's admission. Could Dan have had an alien contact that he was not aware of? The psychologist had often worked with people whose memories of such encounters lay buried deep in their subconscious minds. With the help of hypnosis, those memories had been brought to the surface.

Dan readily agreed to explore the possibility that he had had such an encounter. But neither he nor the doctor expected to discover that Dan himself was an alien from outer space!

Under hypnosis Dan "remembered" that before he came to Earth, during what he called the "old days," he had been a crew member of a mile-and-a-half-long spaceship assigned to "planetary control." It was a job he relished. Dan recalled that ship life was "a lot of fun," with many parties and socializing among the 3,500 men and women on board. The people had humanlike bodies and ate food similar to Earth food, including meat, fruit, and vegetables. Each crew member's small personal quarters on the ship held a single bed, storage area, and a movielike screen that provided entertainment.

Ship life was fairly routine until it was time to get back into training. Every two to four weeks the crew was notified of an enemy attack. They were briefed about the enemy, including such information as the weapons status of the planet, their "level," and "what to shoot and what to leave alone." During an attack the huge ship would plummet through the atmosphere, releasing 14 smaller landing craft. The 100 personnel on each craft used what Dan called "force beam" weaponry to threaten or kill the enemy. As captain of one of the landing craft, Dan considered the attacks "kind of fun."

A tour of duty aboard the ship lasted a year, after which time the crew was sent back to a station in space for "shore leave" before returning for another year of duty. After many such tours, Dan was eventually "retired" to the planet Earth. Retirement was a process in which his physical body remained on board the ship while his mind was able to enter another body of his choice. In Dan's case, he replaced a small boy living in the state of Washington. At first, Dan had a confusion of memories—both his own and the young boy's—and he felt some regrets about never being able to return home. Eventually, however, memories of his past life faded, and to all intents and purposes, Dan became an Earthling.

But at the age of 14 his past came back to haunt him in the form of a frightening alien visitor. While he was waiting for the bus in front of his school, a face appeared in his mind, a familiar but horrible nonhuman face that Dan recognized as one of the "treacherous" ones. Dan knew the visitor wanted information, but he was unable to remember what questions had been asked, since the creature took that part of Dan's memory away. Upset by the experience, Dan knew he could not defend himself against such a powerful enemy.

Two weeks later Dan had a more welcome mental encounter with his old captain, a good friend. Knowing that he was breaking the rules by contacting Dan during his retirement, the captain warned his former crew member about talking to the treacherous ones.

Not all Dan's alien encounters were mental, however. A nonviolent humanoid he called one of the "intellectuals" arrived at the front door of Dan's house wearing a silver suit that covered his brown skin. He had rather large hooded eyes, a small mouth and nose, and a slight build. After chatting with Dan for some time about his attitude toward living on Earth, the visitor left. During a second visit the humanoid took what Dan considered to be useless printouts from his computer.

During still another encounter, Dan was transported back aboard his old spaceship, where he was reunited with friends who joked about his blue jeans and cowboy boots. Dan realized how much he missed his old way of life. He and his friend the captain discussed the need for experienced people like Dan to carry out a major operation—the destruction of a planet. But before they could finalize their plans, Dan suddenly found himself back in his own home.

Now that Dan has fully "explored" his memory of his past life, he thinks his life on Earth may be in limbo. Since his last visit aboard his old spaceship on August 15, 1987, he has had no further word about whether the rules could be broken to allow his return to space. But given the chance to return, Dan would not hesitate.

"I want to go back," he told Dr. Fiore. "It's just so far superior to be there than to be here. And I know that if I were there, I'd be involved in something so grand, that what happens here means nothing. . . . To be back, to be able to do that again, would be fabulous!" ∎

*If you have been timed while reading this selection, enter your reading time below. Then turn to the Words-per-Minute table on page 155 and look up your reading speed (words per minute). Enter your reading speed on the graph on page 156.*

READING TIME: Unit 20

_____ : _____
*Minutes*      *Seconds*

# How well did you read?

- *Answer the four types of questions that follow. The directions for each type of question tell you how to mark your answers.*

- *When you have finished all four exercises, check your work by using the answer key on page 152. For each right answer, put a check mark ( ✓ ) on the line beside the box. For each wrong answer, write the correct answer on the line.*

- *For scoring each exercise, follow the directions below the questions.*

## A  FINDING THE MAIN IDEA

Look at the three statements below. One expresses the main idea of the story you just read. A good main idea statement answers two questions: it tells *who* or *what* is the subject of the story, and it answers the understood question *does what?* or *is what?* Another statement is *too broad;* it is vague and doesn't tell much about the topic of the story. The third statement is *too narrow;* it tells about only one part of the story.

Match the statements with the three answer choices below by writing the letter of each answer in the box in front of the statement it goes with.

**M—Main Idea**     **B—Too Broad**     **N—Too Narrow**

_____ ☐ 1. Like others who claim to have had UFO encounters, Dan explored his earlier life through hypnosis.

_____ ☐ 2. Through hypnosis Dan recalled his past life on board a spaceship.

_____ ☐ 3. Before he "retired" to Earth as a human, Dan was the captain of an alien spaceship.

_____ Score 15 points for a correct *M* answer

_____ Score 5 points for each correct *B* or *N* answer

_____ TOTAL SCORE: Finding the Main Idea

## B RECALLING FACTS

How well do you remember the facts in the story you just read? Put an *x* in the box in front of the correct answer to each of the multiple-choice questions below.

1. Through hypnosis Dan learns
   - ☐ a. about his former life.
   - ☐ b. how to deal with his nightmares.
   - ☐ c. to recognize UFOs.

2. Dan came to Earth because
   - ☐ a. his spaceship crashed here.
   - ☐ b. he was chosen to retire here.
   - ☐ c. he has fond memories of the planet.

3. Before coming to Earth, Dan was a
   - ☐ a. licensed airplane pilot.
   - ☐ b. teacher.
   - ☐ c. captain of a spaceship.

4. Dan's extraterrestrial friends
   - ☐ a. had humanlike bodies.
   - ☐ b. were all intellectuals.
   - ☐ c. were jealous of his new life.

5. Given the chance to return home, Dan would
   - ☐ a. stay on Earth.
   - ☐ b. not hesitate.
   - ☐ c. think twice.

Score 5 points for each correct answer

_____ TOTAL SCORE: Recalling Facts

## C MAKING INFERENCES

An inference is a judgment that is made or an idea that is arrived at based on facts or on information that is given. You make an inference when you understand something that is *not* stated directly but that is *implied,* or suggested, by the facts that are given.

Below are five statements that are judgments or ideas that have been arrived at from the facts of the story. Write the letter *C* in the box in front of each statement that is a correct inference. Write the letter *F* in front of each faulty inference.

**C—Correct Inference      F—Faulty Inference**

1. Dan's interest in UFOs was the result of his past life.

2. If not for hypnosis, Dan would probably not have remembered his past life.

3. Dr. Fiore seemed frightened by Dan's stories of the "old days."

4. Dan's spaceship experience would have prepared him for military service on Earth.

5. Dan comes from a peace-loving planet.

Score 5 points for each correct answer

_____ TOTAL SCORE: Making Inferences

## D USING WORDS PRECISELY

Each of the numbered sentences below contains an underlined word or phrase from the story you have just read. Under the sentence are three definitions. One is a *synonym,* a word that means the same or almost the same thing: *big* and *large.* One is an *antonym,* a word that has the opposite or nearly opposite meaning: *love* and *hate.* One is an unrelated word; it has a completely *different* meaning. Match the definitions with the three answer choices by writing the letter that stands for each answer in the box in front of the definition it goes with.

**S—Synonym     A—Antonym     D—Different**

1. "I try to remain open and <u>objective</u> [about UFOs]."

____    ☐ a. creative

____    ☐ b. open-minded

____    ☐ c. unfair

2. "Every time I look at the night sky, I have a <u>nostalgic</u> feeling. . . ."

____    ☐ a. longing

____    ☐ b. romantic

____    ☐ c. content

3. Dr. Edith Fiore's eyes widened as she heard Dan's <u>admission</u>.

____    ☐ a. entrance

____    ☐ b. admitting to be true

____    ☐ c. denial

4. During an attack the huge ship would <u>plummet</u> through the atmosphere, releasing 14 smaller landing craft.

____    ☐ a. drop sharply

____    ☐ b. soar quickly

____    ☐ c. move heavily

5. He had rather large <u>hooded</u> eyes, a small mouth and nose, and a slight build.

____    ☐ a. gaping

____    ☐ b. savage

____    ☐ c. half-closed

____    Score 3 points for each correct *S* answer

____    Score 1 point for each correct *A* or *D* answer

____    TOTAL SCORE: Using Words Precisely

● *Enter the four total scores in the spaces below, and add them together to find your Critical Reading Score. Then record your Critical Reading Score on the graph on page 157.*

_____    Finding the Main Idea
_____    Recalling Facts
_____    Making Inferences
_____    Using Words Precisely
_____    **CRITICAL READING SCORE:  Unit 20**

The Russian city of Voronezh seems an unlikely place for UFO sightings. But from September 21 to October 7, 1989, thousands of people claimed to have seen UFOs. On September 27 witnesses said a UFO landed in a city park, and a giant alien with three eyes emerged! With the alien was a robot. People screamed in fear at the creatures, when suddenly the aliens and the spacecraft disappeared.

# The Russian Giants

When the rest of the world first got wind of the bizarre UFO incident that had occurred in the Russian city of Voronezh, people were understandably skeptical. After all, according to the Western press the witnesses were just "a bunch of kids." And the aliens they claimed to have seen had huge bodies and tiny heads—just the opposite of most Western alien descriptions. The news reports, however, lacked crucial information. Not only "kids," but also approximately 40 adults witnessed the strange occurrence in Voronezh. And scientists found physical evidence at the site that was difficult to dispute.

Here is what happened. On September 27, 1989, around 6:30 in the evening, Vasya Surin and his friend, Genya Blinov, were playing soccer in a park when they noticed an unusual pinkish light in the sky. As the light grew closer, it became a bright red sphere about 30 feet in diameter. The sphere circled about 40 feet above the ground and then suddenly flew away.

It was not long before the UFO returned, hovering closer to the ground. By this time a crowd had joined the children, and everyone watched in awe as a hatch in the bottom of the sphere opened. A giant loomed in the opening, scanned the ground below, then closed the hatch. The sphere dropped lower, permanently bending a poplar tree in its path.

Finally the UFO landed. On the ground it seemed to measure about 45 feet by 19 feet. Once again the hatch opened, and a giant alien about 10 feet tall emerged, dressed in silver overalls and bronze-colored boots. Its face was dominated by three eyes. Two of the eyes were whitish, while the third, in the middle, was red and lacked a pupil. There was a disk-shaped object on the being's chest. With the giant alien was something that looked like a robot. When the giant adjusted a dial on the robot's chest, it started to walk mechanically.

One of the witnesses, a young boy, cried out, only to be immediately silenced by a look from the giant alien's eyes, which seemed to emit a strange glow. Suddenly everyone started shouting. Even more suddenly, the sphere and the aliens vanished.

After a short time the sphere and the alien returned. The giant carried a tube about four feet long. It pointed the tube at a boy who was nearby, and the teenager disappeared. The demonstration apparently complete, the alien then reentered the sphere, which zoomed away. At the same instant, the boy reappeared.

Had this incident had fewer witnesses, investigators might have dismissed the weird story as just a fantasy. But the number of eyewitnesses, coupled with the physical evidence, made the whole incident difficult to ignore. In addition to the bent tree, grass in the area where the UFO was reported to have landed was badly burned. Scientists measured a 60-foot diameter depression, within which were four deep dents thought to be marks from landing gear. Using special instruments, scientists reconstructed a path the aliens followed from their craft. Witnesses unaware of these findings later confirmed the same path.

Then there were the many other UFO sightings elsewhere in Voronezh. From September 21 to October 7, thousands of people claimed to have seen a UFO. The report from Yuli Nikanorovich Sviridov, an engineer, was typical.

Around 8:00 P.M., on September 27, from the fourth-floor balcony, I saw a big, bright red sphere move between the houses at an altitude of a thousand feet. [It had] a crimson halo along the edges. Its speed was comparable to that of a small plane.

Over 30 people witnessed UFO landings in Voronezh. Their reports were remarkably similar. A small metal ladder appeared from an open hatch. Giant aliens emerged, carrying a robot that later walked mechanically when "turned on." After a few minutes of walking about, the robot returned to the giants, who turned it off and carried it back

**143**

into the sphere. The ladder retracted automatically, the hatch closed, and the UFO zoomed away.

One of the most unusual of the Voronezh episodes was reported by M. N. Polyakov, a 56-year-old factory worker. Polyakov and a friend were driving toward the city one day in late September when the car suddenly experienced an electrical blackout. The car's headlights and radio died, followed by the engine, which refused to restart. When Polyakov's friend tried to light a cigarette, the matches would not ignite. Then the men became aware of a pinkish-yellow sphere shining dimly above the road. The sphere sent down a beam that moved toward the car. When the beam scanned the car's hood, the engine started to smoke. Polyakov recalled that "the car moved and something appeared on the driver's seat. I sensed an alien presence; I felt that I could stretch my arm and touch the invisible being. And although my brain and willpower ordered my hand to touch the unpleasant thing, I could not move my arm."

Finally, much to Polyakov's relief, the beam moved away. A few seconds later, the car lights came back on. His friend was able to start the car, but he remained strangely silent. When Polyakov tried to discuss what had happened, his friend could not remember a thing!

Polyakov was at first reluctant to tell his story. "People might think I am a lunatic," he said. "But my friends convinced me."

Why is Voronezh such a hotbed of UFO activity? Investigators are puzzled. At first glance, this large city seems an unlikely spot for UFO sightings. About 300 miles south of Moscow, it is home to nearly a million people. Its industries include machinery, electrical products, chemicals, cigarettes, and processed foods.

According to UFO researcher Alexander Mosolov, "the center of the activity varies within the city of Voronezh itself. It moves from the park to the power plant. Many of the sightings seem to occur in polluted areas. The park itself used to be a garbage dump. It was covered over with dirt and replanted. Similarly, the electrical plant and the site of the future nuclear plant have been visited." Armed with this information, Mosolov is still frustrated. "We do not know what all this means," he said.

No one knows for sure "what all this means." But if we on Earth are not alone in this universe, could it be that those who share it with us have a vested interest in our future? Perhaps "what all this means" is a simple message from our extraterrestrial neighbors: "Treat your planet kindly, for what you do on Earth will affect us all." ■

*If you have been timed while reading this selection, enter your reading time below. Then turn to the Words-per-Minute table on page 155 and look up your reading speed (words per minute). Enter your reading speed on the graph on page 156.*

READING TIME: Unit 21

_____ : _____
*Minutes*     *Seconds*

# How well did you read?

- *Answer the four types of questions that follow. The directions for each type of question tell you how to mark your answers.*

- *When you have finished all four exercises, check your work by using the answer key on page 152. For each right answer, put a check mark (✓) on the line beside the box. For each wrong answer, write the correct answer on the line.*

- *For scoring each exercise, follow the directions below the questions.*

## A  FINDING THE MAIN IDEA

Look at the three statements below. One expresses the main idea of the story you just read. A good main idea statement answers two questions: it tells *who* or *what* is the subject of the story, and it answers the understood question *does what?* or *is what?* Another statement is *too broad;* it is vague and doesn't tell much about the topic of the story. The third statement is *too narrow;* it tells about only one part of the story.

Match the statements with the three answer choices below by writing the letter of each answer in the box in front of the statement it goes with.

**M—Main Idea      B—Too Broad      N—Too Narrow**

____ ☐ 1. On September 27, 1989, Vasya Surin and Genya Blinov witnessed a UFO landing in a park in Voronezh.

____ ☐ 2. The Russian city of Voronezh became a center of UFO activity in the fall of 1989.

____ ☐ 3. Investigators don't know why certain regions of the world become centers of UFO activity.

____ Score 15 points for a correct *M* answer
____ Score 5 points for each correct *B* or *N* answer

____ TOTAL SCORE:  Finding the Main Idea

## B  RECALLING FACTS

How well do you remember the facts in the story you just read?
Put an x in the box in front of the correct answer to each of the
multiple-choice questions below.

1. Voronezh is
   - [ ] a. the largest city in Russia.
   - [ ] b. a large industrial center.
   - [ ] c. a small village.

2. The alien beings seen in Voronezh
   - [ ] a. are typical of those seen in the West.
   - [ ] b. had small bodies and large heads.
   - [ ] c. had huge bodies with small heads.

3. Most UFO sightings in Voronezh involved
   - [ ] a. a bright red sphere.
   - [ ] b. a cigar-shaped craft.
   - [ ] c. objects that resembled small planes.

4. Investigators of the Voronezh incidents were impressed by
   - [ ] a. reports from reliable witnesses.
   - [ ] b. the timing of eyewitness reports.
   - [ ] c. stories in the Western news.

5. UFO activity in Voronezh occurred
   - [ ] a. at random.
   - [ ] b. near tall buildings.
   - [ ] c. frequently in polluted areas.

Score 5 points for each correct answer

_____ TOTAL SCORE: Recalling Facts

## C  MAKING INFERENCES

An inference is a judgment that is made or an idea that is arrived
at based on facts or on information that is given. You make an
inference when you understand something that is *not* stated
directly but that is *implied,* or suggested, by the facts that are given.

Below are five statements that are judgments or ideas that have
been arrived at from the facts of the story. Write the letter C in
the box in front of each statement that is a correct inference. Write
the letter F in front of each faulty inference.

**C—Correct Inference     F—Faulty Inference**

- [ ] 1. The crowd had gathered at the park to welcome the UFO's arrival.

- [ ] 2. The Western press does a poor job of reporting news events in Russia.

- [ ] 3. Voronezh may have been chosen as a UFO center because its industry endangers the atmosphere.

- [ ] 4. UFOs are seen most often in large industrial cities.

- [ ] 5. The Russian giants were probably a figment of people's imagination.

Score 5 points for each correct answer

_____ TOTAL SCORE: Making Inferences

## D USING WORDS PRECISELY

Each of the numbered sentences below contains an underlined word or phrase from the story you have just read. Under the sentence are three definitions. One is a *synonym*, a word that means the same or almost the same thing: *big* and *large*. One is an *antonym*, a word that has the opposite or nearly opposite meaning: *love* and *hate*. One is an unrelated word; it has a completely *different* meaning. Match the definitions with the three answer choices by writing the letter that stands for each answer in the box in front of the definition it goes with.

**S—Synonym     A—Antonym     D—Different**

1. The news reports, however, lacked <u>crucial</u> information.

____ ☐ a. important

____ ☐ b. urgent

____ ☐ c. insignificant

2. A giant <u>loomed</u> in the opening, scanned the ground below, then closed the hatch.

____ ☐ a. appeared friendly

____ ☐ b. appeared large and threatening

____ ☐ c. appeared woven

3. Its face was <u>dominated</u> by three eyes.

____ ☐ a. diminished

____ ☐ b. influenced

____ ☐ c. overpowered

4. Why is Voronezh such a <u>hotbed</u> of activity?

____ ☐ a. place where seedlings are grown

____ ☐ b. place of rapid growth or development

____ ☐ c. place of slow growth or development

5. . . . could it be that those who share it [the universe] with us have a <u>vested</u> interest in our future?

____ ☐ a. rightful

____ ☐ b. unlawful

____ ☐ c. financial

____ Score 3 points for each correct *S* answer

____ Score 1 point for each correct *A* or *D* answer

____ TOTAL SCORE: Using Words Precisely

● *Enter the four total scores in the spaces below, and add them together to find your Critical Reading Score. Then record your Critical Reading Score on the graph on page 157.*

_____ Finding the Main Idea
_____ Recalling Facts
_____ Making Inferences
_____ Using Words Precisely
_____ CRITICAL READING SCORE: Unit 21

# ANSWER KEY

## 1 The Roswell Incident
A. Finding the Main Idea
1. M    2. B    3. N
B. Recalling Facts
1. b    2. c    3. c    4. c    5. b
C. Making Inferences
1. F    2. C    3. F    4. F    5. C
D. Using Words Precisely
1.    a. S    b. A    c. D
2.    a. A    b. S    c. D
3.    a. D    b. A    c. S
4.    a. S    b. A    c. D
5.    a. D    b. S    c. A

## 2 The First Contact
A. Finding the Main Idea
1. N    2. B    3. M
B. Recalling Facts
1. a    2. c    3. b    4. a    5. c
C. Making Inferences
1. C    2. C    3. C    4. F    5. C
D. Using Words Precisely
1.    a. S    b. D    c. A
2.    a. A    b. S    c. D
3.    a. D    b. A    c. S
4.    a. S    b. A    c. D
5.    a. A    b. D    c. S

## 3 The Kelly-Hopkinsville Siege
A. Finding the Main Idea
1. N    2. M    3. B
B. Recalling Facts
1. a    2. c    3. c    4. c    5. b
C. Making Inferences
1. F    2. F    3. C    4. C    5. F
D. Using Words Precisely
1.    a. S    b. D    c. A
2.    a. A    b. S    c. D
3.    a. D    b. S    c. A
4.    a. A    b. D    c. S
5.    a. S    b. A    c. D

## 4 An Encounter in New Guinea
A. Finding the Main Idea
1. M    2. N    3. B
B. Recalling Facts
1. c    2. a    3. b    4. a    5. b
C. Making Inferences
1. C    2. F    3. C    4. F    5. F
D. Using Words Precisely
1.    a. S    b. D    c. A
2.    a. D    b. A    c. S
3.    a. A    b. S    c. D
4.    a. D    b. S    c. A
5.    a. S    b. A    c. D

## 5 Aliens on Earth?
A. Finding the Main Idea
1. B    2. N    3. M
B. Recalling Facts
1. a    2. b    3. c    4. c    5. b
C. Making Inferences
1. C    2. F    3. C    4. F    5. C
D. Using Words Precisely
1.    a. S    b. D    c. A
2.    a. A    b. D    c. S
3.    a. S    b. A    c. D
4.    a. D    b. S    c. A
5.    a. D    b. A    c. S

## 6 The Socorro Sighting
A. Finding the Main Idea
1. N    2. B    3. M
B. Recalling Facts
1. c    2. c    3. a    4. a    5. b
C. Making Inferences
1. C    2. F    3. C    4. C    5. F
D. Using Words Precisely
1.    a. A    b. D    c. S
2.    a. D    b. S    c. A
3.    a. D    b. A    c. S
4.    a. D    b. S    c. A
5.    a. S    b. D    c. A

## 7 Incident at Exeter
A. Finding the Main Idea
1. M    2. B    3. N
B. Recalling Facts
1. b    2. b    3. b    4. c    5. c
C. Making Inferences
1. C    2. C    3. F    4. C    5. F
D. Using Words Precisely
1.    a. A    b. S    c. D
2.    a. S    b. A    c. D
3.    a. D    b. S    c. A
4.    a. S    b. D    c. A
5.    a. A    b. D    c. S

## 8 Kim's Story
A. Finding the Main Idea
1. **B**  2. **M**  3. **N**
B. Recalling Facts
1. **b**  2. **b**  3. **b**  4. **a**  5. **c**
C. Making Inferences
1. **F**  2. **C**  3. **F**  4. **C**  5. **C**
D. Using Words Precisely
1. a. **S**  b. **A**  c. **D**
2. a. **A**  b. **S**  c. **D**
3. a. **D**  b. **A**  c. **S**
4. a. **A**  b. **D**  c. **S**
5. a. **S**  b. **D**  c. **A**

## 9 The Secrets of Betty Andreasson
A. Finding the Main Idea
1. **B**  2. **N**  3. **M**
B. Recalling Facts
1. **a**  2. **c**  3. **b**  4. **a**  5. **b**
C. Making Inferences
1. **C**  2. **F**  3. **F**  4. **F**  5. **C**
D. Using Words Precisely
1. a. **S**  b. **A**  c. **D**
2. a. **A**  b. **D**  c. **S**
3. a. **S**  b. **D**  c. **A**
4. a. **D**  b. **A**  c. **S**
5. a. **D**  b. **S**  c. **A**

## 10 Encounter in Nebraska
A. Finding the Main Idea
1. **N**  2. **M**  3. **B**
B. Recalling Facts
1. **b**  2. **c**  3. **a**  4. **c**  5. **a**
C. Making Inferences
1. **F**  2. **C**  3. **F**  4. **C**  5. **F**
D. Using Words Precisely
1. a. **D**  b. **A**  c. **S**
2. a. **A**  b. **D**  c. **S**
3. a. **S**  b. **A**  c. **D**
4. a. **S**  b. **D**  c. **A**
5. a. **A**  b. **S**  c. **D**

## 11 Dr. X Finds a Cure
A. Finding the Main Idea
1. **M**  2. **N**  3. **B**
B. Recalling Facts
1. **c**  2. **b**  3. **b**  4. **a**  5. **c**
C. Making Inferences
1. **F**  2. **C**  3. **C**  4. **F**  5. **C**
D. Using Words Precisely
1. a. **D**  b. **S**  c. **A**
2. a. **D**  b. **A**  c. **S**
3. a. **D**  b. **S**  c. **A**
4. a. **A**  b. **D**  c. **S**
5. a. **S**  b. **A**  c. **D**

## 12 The Delphos Ring
A. Finding the Main Idea
1. **B**  2. **N**  3. **M**
B. Recalling Facts
1. **c**  2. **c**  3. **b**  4. **c**  5. **b**
C. Making Inferences
1. **F**  2. **C**  3. **F**  4. **C**  5. **C**
D. Using Words Precisely
1. a. **A**  b. **S**  c. **D**
2. a. **D**  b. **S**  c. **A**
3. a. **S**  b. **A**  c. **D**
4. a. **D**  b. **A**  c. **S**
5. a. **S**  b. **D**  c. **A**

## 13 The Pascagoula Encounter
A. Finding the Main Idea
1. **M**  2. **B**  3. **N**
B. Recalling Facts
1. **c**  2. **a**  3. **a**  4. **c**  5. **c**
C. Making Inferences
1. **C**  2. **F**  3. **F**  4. **C**  5. **F**
D. Using Words Precisely
1. a. **A**  b. **D**  c. **S**
2. a. **S**  b. **A**  c. **D**
3. a. **D**  b. **A**  c. **S**
4. a. **S**  b. **A**  c. **D**
5. a. **A**  b. **S**  c. **D**

## 14 The Beit Bridge Encounter
A. Finding the Main Idea
1. **M**  2. **N**  3. **B**
B. Recalling Facts
1. **b**  2. **a**  3. **b**  4. **b**  5. **c**
C. Making Inferences
1. **C**  2. **F**  3. **F**  4. **F**  5. **C**
D. Using Words Precisely
1. a. **D**  b. **S**  c. **A**
2. a. **S**  b. **A**  c. **D**
3. a. **A**  b. **D**  c. **S**
4. a. **S**  b. **D**  c. **A**
5. a. **D**  b. **A**  c. **S**

## 15 The Wave That Hit Sweden
A. Finding the Main Idea
1. B    2. M    3. N
B. Recalling Facts
1. b    2. a    3. b    4. c    5. a
C. Making Inferences
1. C    2. C    3. F    4. F    5. C
D. Using Words Precisely
1. a. S    b. A    c. D
2. a. S    b. D    c. A
3. a. A    b. S    c. D
4. a. D    b. S    c. A
5. a. D    b. A    c. S

## 16 The Woodcutter's Tale
A. Finding the Main Idea
1. N    2. M    3. B
B. Recalling Facts
1. c    2. b    3. a    4. b    5. c
C. Making Inferences
1. F    2. C    3. F    4. C    5. C
D. Using Words Precisely
1. a. S    b. A    c. D
2. a. D    b. A    c. S
3. a. S    b. D    c. A
4. a. A    b. D    c. S
5. a. A    b. S    c. D

## 17 The Mysterious Men in Black
A. Finding the Main Idea
1. M    2. B    3. N
B. Recalling Facts
1. c    2. b    3. b    4. a    5. a
C. Making Inferences
1. C    2. F    3. F    4. C    5. C
D. Using Words Precisely
1. a. D    b. A    c. S
2. a. A    b. S    c. D
3. a. S    b. D    c. A
4. a. A    b. D    c. S
5. a. D    b. S    c. A

## 18 The Chosen One
A. Finding the Main Idea
1. B    2. N    3. M
B. Recalling Facts
1. a    2. a    3. c    4. b    5. b
C. Making Inferences
1. F    2. C    3. C    4. C    5. C
D. Using Words Precisely
1. a. D    b. A    c. S
2. a. S    b. A    c. D
3. a. A    b. D    c. S
4. a. S    b. D    c. A
5. a. D    b. S    c. A

## 19 The Human Experiment
A. Finding the Main Idea
1. M    2. N    3. B
B. Recalling Facts
1. b    2. b    3. c    4. a    5. a
C. Making Inferences
1. C    2. F    3. F    4. C    5. C
D. Using Words Precisely
1. a. S    b. A    c. D
2. a. A    b. D    c. S
3. a. D    b. S    c. A
4. a. A    b. S    c. D
5. a. S    b. D    c. A

## 20 At Home in Space
A. Finding the Main Idea
1. B    2. M    3. N
B. Recalling Facts
1. a    2. b    3. c    4. a    5. b
C. Making Inferences
1. C    2. C    3. F    4. C    5. F
D. Using Words Precisely
1. a. D    b. S    c. A
2. a. S    b. D    c. A
3. a. D    b. S    c. A
4. a. S    b. A    c. D
5. a. A    b. D    c. S

## 21 The Russian Giants
A. Finding the Main Idea
1. N    2. M    3. B
B. Recalling Facts
1. b    2. c    3. a    4. a    5. c
C. Making Inferences
1. C    2. F    3. C    4. F    5. F
D. Using Words Precisely
1. a. S    b. D    c. A
2. a. A    b. S    c. D
3. a. A    b. D    c. S
4. a. D    b. S    c. A
5. a. S    b. A    c. D

# WORDS-PER-MINUTE TABLE
# & PROGRESS GRAPHS

# Words per Minute

| Unit ▶ | Sample | 1 | 2 | 3 | 4 | 5 | 6 | 7 | |
|---|---|---|---|---|---|---|---|---|---|
| No. of Words ▶ | 894 | 1057 | 1269 | 869 | 810 | 838 | 1127 | 1125 | |
| 1:30 | 596 | 704 | 846 | 579 | 540 | 558 | 751 | 750 | 90 |
| 1:40 | 538 | 636 | 764 | 523 | 487 | 504 | 678 | 677 | 100 |
| 1:50 | 488 | 577 | 693 | 474 | 442 | 457 | 615 | 614 | 110 |
| 2:00 | 447 | 528 | 634 | 434 | 405 | 419 | 563 | 562 | 120 |
| 2:10 | 413 | 489 | 587 | 402 | 375 | 387 | 521 | 520 | 130 |
| 2:20 | 383 | 453 | 544 | 372 | 347 | 359 | 483 | 482 | 140 |
| 2:30 | 357 | 422 | 507 | 347 | 324 | 335 | 450 | 450 | 150 |
| 2:40 | 336 | 397 | 477 | 326 | 304 | 315 | 423 | 422 | 160 |
| 2:50 | 315 | 373 | 448 | 307 | 286 | 296 | 398 | 397 | 170 |
| 3:00 | 298 | 352 | 423 | 289 | 270 | 279 | 375 | 375 | 180 |
| 3:10 | 282 | 334 | 401 | 275 | 256 | 265 | 356 | 356 | 190 |
| 3:20 | 268 | 317 | 381 | 260 | 243 | 251 | 338 | 337 | 200 |
| 3:30 | 255 | 302 | 362 | 248 | 231 | 239 | 322 | 321 | 210 |
| 3:40 | 244 | 288 | 346 | 237 | 221 | 228 | 307 | 307 | 220 |
| 3:50 | 233 | 275 | 331 | 226 | 211 | 218 | 294 | 293 | 230 |
| 4:00 | 223 | 264 | 317 | 217 | 202 | 209 | 281 | 281 | 240 |
| 4:10 | 214 | 254 | 305 | 208 | 194 | 201 | 270 | 270 | 250 |
| 4:20 | 206 | 244 | 293 | 200 | 187 | 193 | 260 | 259 | 260 |
| 4:30 | 198 | 234 | 282 | 193 | 180 | 186 | 250 | 250 | 270 |
| 4:40 | 191 | 226 | 272 | 186 | 173 | 179 | 241 | 241 | 280 |
| 4:50 | 185 | 218 | 262 | 179 | 167 | 173 | 233 | 232 | 290 |
| 5:00 | 178 | 211 | 253 | 173 | 162 | 167 | 225 | 225 | 300 |
| 5:10 | 173 | 204 | 245 | 168 | 156 | 162 | 218 | 218 | 310 |
| 5:20 | 167 | 198 | 238 | 163 | 151 | 157 | 211 | 211 | 320 |
| 5:30 | 162 | 192 | 230 | 158 | 147 | 152 | 204 | 204 | 330 |
| 5:40 | 157 | 186 | 224 | 153 | 143 | 148 | 199 | 198 | 340 |
| 5:50 | 153 | 181 | 217 | 149 | 138 | 143 | 193 | 192 | 350 |
| 6:00 | 149 | 176 | 211 | 144 | 135 | 139 | 187 | 187 | 360 |
| 6:10 | 145 | 171 | 206 | 141 | 131 | 136 | 182 | 182 | 370 |
| 6:20 | 141 | 166 | 200 | 137 | 127 | 132 | 178 | 177 | 380 |
| 6:30 | 137 | 162 | 195 | 133 | 124 | 128 | 173 | 173 | 390 |
| 6:40 | 134 | 158 | 190 | 130 | 121 | 125 | 169 | 168 | 400 |
| 6:50 | 130 | 154 | 185 | 127 | 118 | 122 | 165 | 164 | 410 |
| 7:00 | 127 | 151 | 181 | 124 | 115 | 119 | 161 | 160 | 420 |
| 7:20 | 121 | 144 | 173 | 118 | 110 | 114 | 153 | 153 | 440 |
| 7:40 | 116 | 137 | 165 | 113 | 105 | 109 | 147 | 146 | 460 |
| 8:00 | 111 | 132 | 158 | 108 | 101 | 104 | 140 | 140 | 480 |

Minutes and Seconds ▶

Seconds ◀

## GROUP TWO

| Unit ▶ | 8 | 9 | 10 | 11 | 12 | 13 | 14 | |
|---|---|---|---|---|---|---|---|---|
| No. of Words ▶ | 850 | 1011 | 892 | 830 | 1035 | 1077 | 1115 | |
| 1:30 | 566 | 674 | 594 | 553 | 690 | 718 | 743 | 90 |
| 1:40 | 512 | 609 | 537 | 500 | 623 | 648 | 671 | 100 |
| 1:50 | 464 | 552 | 487 | 453 | 565 | 588 | 609 | 110 |
| 2:00 | 425 | 505 | 446 | 415 | 517 | 538 | 557 | 120 |
| 2:10 | 393 | 468 | 412 | 384 | 479 | 498 | 516 | 130 |
| 2:20 | 364 | 433 | 382 | 356 | 444 | 462 | 478 | 140 |
| 2:30 | 340 | 404 | 356 | 332 | 414 | 430 | 446 | 150 |
| 2:40 | 319 | 380 | 335 | 312 | 389 | 404 | 419 | 160 |
| 2:50 | 300 | 357 | 315 | 293 | 365 | 380 | 393 | 170 |
| 3:00 | 283 | 337 | 297 | 276 | 345 | 359 | 371 | 180 |
| 3:10 | 268 | 319 | 282 | 262 | 327 | 340 | 352 | 190 |
| 3:20 | 255 | 303 | 267 | 249 | 310 | 323 | 334 | 200 |
| 3:30 | 242 | 288 | 254 | 237 | 295 | 307 | 318 | 210 |
| 3:40 | 232 | 276 | 243 | 226 | 282 | 294 | 304 | 220 |
| 3:50 | 221 | 263 | 232 | 216 | 270 | 281 | 291 | 230 |
| 4:00 | 212 | 252 | 223 | 207 | 258 | 269 | 278 | 240 |
| 4:10 | 204 | 243 | 214 | 199 | 248 | 258 | 268 | 250 |
| 4:20 | 196 | 233 | 206 | 191 | 239 | 248 | 257 | 260 |
| 4:30 | 188 | 224 | 198 | 184 | 230 | 239 | 247 | 270 |
| 4:40 | 182 | 216 | 191 | 178 | 222 | 231 | 239 | 280 |
| 4:50 | 175 | 209 | 184 | 171 | 214 | 222 | 230 | 290 |
| 5:00 | 170 | 202 | 178 | 166 | 207 | 215 | 223 | 300 |
| 5:10 | 164 | 195 | 172 | 160 | 200 | 208 | 216 | 310 |
| 5:20 | 159 | 189 | 167 | 155 | 194 | 202 | 209 | 320 |
| 5:30 | 154 | 183 | 162 | 150 | 188 | 195 | 202 | 330 |
| 5:40 | 150 | 178 | 157 | 146 | 182 | 190 | 196 | 340 |
| 5:50 | 145 | 173 | 153 | 142 | 177 | 184 | 191 | 350 |
| 6:00 | 141 | 168 | 148 | 138 | 172 | 179 | 185 | 360 |
| 6:10 | 137 | 164 | 144 | 134 | 168 | 174 | 181 | 370 |
| 6:20 | 134 | 159 | 140 | 131 | 163 | 170 | 176 | 380 |
| 6:30 | 130 | 155 | 137 | 127 | 159 | 165 | 171 | 390 |
| 6:40 | 127 | 151 | 133 | 124 | 155 | 161 | 167 | 400 |
| 6:50 | 124 | 148 | 130 | 121 | 151 | 157 | 163 | 410 |
| 7:00 | 121 | 144 | 127 | 118 | 147 | 153 | 159 | 420 |
| 7:20 | 115 | 137 | 121 | 113 | 141 | 146 | 152 | 440 |
| 7:40 | 110 | 131 | 116 | 108 | 135 | 140 | 145 | 460 |
| 8:00 | 106 | 126 | 111 | 103 | 129 | 134 | 139 | 480 |

*Minutes and Seconds* (left axis) — *Seconds* (right axis)

## GROUP THREE

| Unit ▶ | 15 | 16 | 17 | 18 | 19 | 20 | 21 | |
|---|---|---|---|---|---|---|---|---|
| No. of Words ▶ | 929 | 1036 | 1229 | 1166 | 1275 | 927 | 1103 | |
| 1:30 | 619 | 690 | 819 | 777 | 850 | 618 | 735 | 90 |
| 1:40 | 559 | 624 | 740 | 702 | 768 | 558 | 664 | 100 |
| 1:50 | 507 | 566 | 671 | 637 | 696 | 506 | 602 | 110 |
| 2:00 | 464 | 518 | 614 | 583 | 637 | 463 | 551 | 120 |
| 2:10 | 430 | 479 | 568 | 539 | 590 | 429 | 510 | 130 |
| 2:20 | 398 | 444 | 527 | 500 | 547 | 397 | 473 | 140 |
| 2:30 | 371 | 414 | 491 | 466 | 510 | 370 | 441 | 150 |
| 2:40 | 349 | 389 | 462 | 438 | 479 | 348 | 414 | 160 |
| 2:50 | 328 | 366 | 434 | 412 | 450 | 327 | 389 | 170 |
| 3:00 | 309 | 345 | 409 | 388 | 425 | 309 | 367 | 180 |
| 3:10 | 293 | 327 | 388 | 368 | 403 | 293 | 349 | 190 |
| 3:20 | 278 | 311 | 369 | 350 | 382 | 278 | 331 | 200 |
| 3:30 | 265 | 296 | 351 | 333 | 364 | 264 | 315 | 210 |
| 3:40 | 253 | 283 | 335 | 318 | 348 | 253 | 301 | 220 |
| 3:50 | 242 | 270 | 320 | 304 | 332 | 242 | 287 | 230 |
| 4:00 | 232 | 259 | 307 | 291 | 318 | 231 | 275 | 240 |
| 4:10 | 223 | 249 | 295 | 280 | 306 | 222 | 265 | 250 |
| 4:20 | 214 | 239 | 283 | 269 | 294 | 214 | 254 | 260 |
| 4:30 | 206 | 230 | 273 | 259 | 283 | 206 | 245 | 270 |
| 4:40 | 199 | 222 | 263 | 250 | 273 | 198 | 236 | 280 |
| 4:50 | 192 | 214 | 254 | 241 | 263 | 191 | 228 | 290 |
| 5:00 | 185 | 207 | 245 | 233 | 255 | 185 | 220 | 300 |
| 5:10 | 180 | 200 | 238 | 225 | 247 | 179 | 213 | 310 |
| 5:20 | 174 | 194 | 230 | 218 | 239 | 173 | 206 | 320 |
| 5:30 | 168 | 188 | 223 | 212 | 231 | 168 | 200 | 330 |
| 5:40 | 164 | 183 | 217 | 206 | 225 | 163 | 194 | 340 |
| 5:50 | 159 | 177 | 210 | 200 | 218 | 159 | 189 | 350 |
| 6:00 | 154 | 172 | 204 | 194 | 212 | 154 | 183 | 360 |
| 6:10 | 150 | 168 | 199 | 189 | 206 | 150 | 179 | 370 |
| 6:20 | 146 | 163 | 194 | 184 | 201 | 146 | 174 | 380 |
| 6:30 | 142 | 159 | 189 | 179 | 196 | 142 | 169 | 390 |
| 6:40 | 139 | 155 | 184 | 175 | 191 | 139 | 165 | 400 |
| 6:50 | 136 | 151 | 179 | 170 | 186 | 135 | 161 | 410 |
| 7:00 | 132 | 148 | 175 | 166 | 182 | 132 | 157 | 420 |
| 7:20 | 126 | 141 | 167 | 159 | 173 | 126 | 150 | 440 |
| 7:40 | 121 | 135 | 160 | 152 | 166 | 121 | 143 | 460 |
| 8:00 | 116 | 129 | 153 | 145 | 159 | 115 | 137 | 480 |

*Minutes and Seconds* (left axis) — *Seconds* (right axis)

# Reading Speed

**Directions:** *Write your Words-per-Minute score for each unit in the box under the number of the unit. Then plot your reading speed on the graph by putting a small* **x** *on the line directly above the number of the unit, across from the number of words per minute you read. As you mark your speed for each unit, graph your progress by drawing a line to connect the* **x**'s.

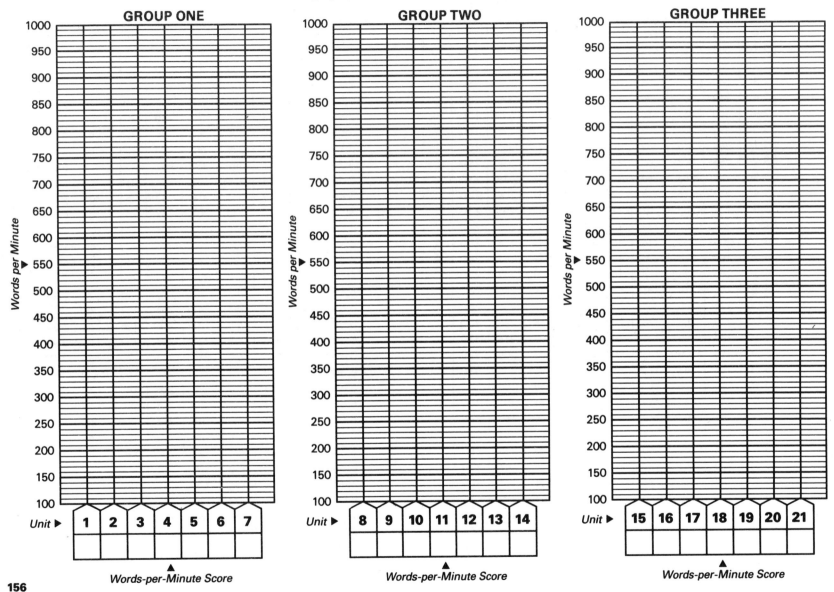

# Critical Reading Scores

**Directions:** *Write your Critical Reading Score for each unit in the box under the number of the unit. Then plot your score on the graph by putting a small* **x** *on the line directly above the number of the unit, across from the score you earned. As you mark your score for each unit, graph your progress by drawing a line to connect the* **x**'s.

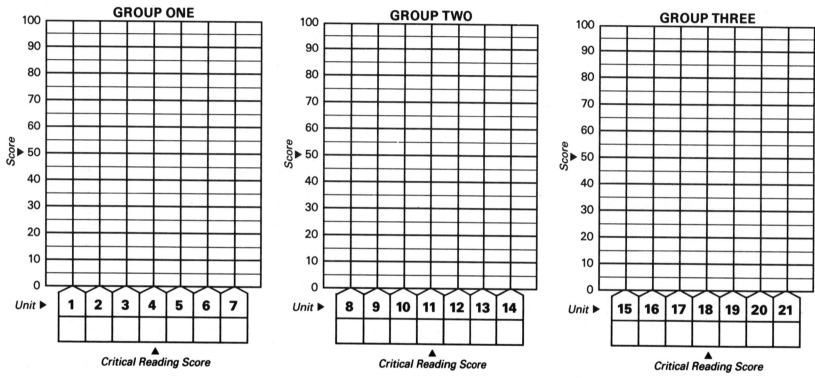

# Picture Credits

Sample Unit: UFO: Fortean Picture Library.
  Newspaper article: The Associated Press

1. Roswell Incident: UPI/Bettmann.
   Newspaper article: Courtesy of Roswell Daily Record

2. First Contact: Mary Evans Picture Library.
   George Adamski: AP/WIDE WORLD PHOTOS

3. Kelly-Hopkinsville: Bob Eggleton

4. New Guinea Encounter: Bob Eggleton

5. Aliens on Earth?: Michael Nicastre

6. Socorro Sighting: Fortean Picture Library

7. Exeter Incident: Photograph courtesy of Ray Fowler.
   Illustration: Bob Eggleton

8. Kim Baker: Photograph by Richard Plummer.
   Kim's drawings: Courtesy of Richard Bonenfant.
   Illustration: Bob Eggleton

9. Betty's Eagle: Courtesy of Ray Fowler.
   Alien: Photograph by George J. Bethoney

10. Nebraska Encounter: Courtesy of Lincoln Journal-Star
    Printing Co.  Alien: All attempts have been made to contact
    Herbert Schirmer

11. Dr. X: Michael Nicastre

12. Delphos Ring: Mutual UFO Network, 103 Oldtowne Road,
    Seguin, TX 78155

13. Pascagoula Encounter: Photri Inc.
    Alien: Fortean Picture Library

14. Beit Bridge: Michael Nicastre

15. UFO Wave in Sweden: Heidi Chang

16. Woodcutter's Tale: Photograph courtesy of Travis Walton.
    Travis confronting aliens: Michael Rogers

17. Men in Black: Mary Evans Picture Library

18. Chosen One: Michael Nicastre

19. Human Experiment: Courtesy of Budd Hopkins

20. At Home in Space: Heidi Chang

21. Russian Giants: Bob Eggleton